FOREIGN POLICY IS YOUR BUSINESS

Theodore R. Weber

CARTOONS BY JIM CRANE

JOHN KNOX PRESS
Richmond, Virginia

Cartoons on pages 17, 50, 51, 76, and 100 are taken from *Inside Out* (Harper and Row Publishers) and used with permission of the artist.

Cartoons on pages 30, 88, 90, 91, and 92 are taken from *On Edge* (John Knox Press). © M. E. Bratcher 1965.

Unless otherwise indicated, Scripture quotations are from the *Revised Standard Version of the Bible,* copyrighted 1946 and 1952.

Library of Congress Cataloging in Publication Data

Weber, Theodore R
Foreign policy is your business.
(Christian ethics for modern man) (Chime paperbacks)
Includes bibliographical references.
1. Christianity and international affairs.
2. U. S.—Foreign relations. I. Title.
BR115.I7W4 261.8'7 74-37769
ISBN 0-8042-9091-1

© John Knox Press 1972
Printed in the United States of America

GENERAL EDITOR'S FOREWORD

Christian Ethics for Modern Man is a series of brief and easy-to-read books on moral issues in contemporary social problems. The books do not provide or pretend to provide the Christian with answers to the complex problems confronting modern man. They do offer guidance to Christians searching for their own answers. The purpose of the series is to help persons make moral judgments more responsibly.

Decisions! Decisions! by George A. Chauncey analyzes the elements that go into any moral judgment and suggests ways one's faith in God can, ought to, and sometimes does influence his moral decisions.

Rich Man Poor Man by Donald W. Shriver, Jr., discusses some of the moral issues American Christians face as they participate in and benefit from the American economy. The book incorporates and comments on recorded conversations among Christian theologians, businessmen, labor leaders, and consumers on those moral issues.

Foreign Policy Is Your Business by Theodore R. Weber examines some of the moral issues faced by a government and its citizens in the development and conduct of foreign policy. Examples: Under what conditions ought a nation go to war? How should the U.S.A. relate to Communist governments? Is it ever right for a government to deceive its own citizens?

These books have been written not only for individual study but also for group discussion. *Leader's Guide to Christian Ethics for Modern Man* by Richard F. Perkins offers valuable suggestions for the use of these books by groups.

George A. Chauncey
GENERAL EDITOR

Preface

Whatever other kind of animal man may be, he is at least a *deciding* animal. His reason discerns and describes the alternatives for action in the broad and narrow dimensions of his situation. His will elects the alternative he prefers to help shape his future. He is not of necessity locked into an automatic process with no options. He makes choices, and he *must* make them. And because he is free—within variable limits—to make choices, he must answer for the uses of his freedom.

The particular context of human decision that concerns us in this book is the foreign policy process of the nation-state, and specifically of the United States of America. We do not need to belabor the importance of that process, because everyone sees on his television screen the effects of it and feels them in his heart, his soul, and his pocketbook. But at the beginning of our inquiry we do need to declare two assumptions about foreign policy decisions that shape our approach to them.

First, they are *moral* decisions. That (obviously!) does not mean that any given foreign policy decision necessarily is morally *right*, but it does mean that every political decision is a form of moral decision inasmuch as it declares one's commitments and discriminates among humanly-affirmed values.

Second, they are *decisions in faith*. What risks shall we elect to take when every available course of action poses threats to our future? Whose interests shall we support when we cannot support everyone's interests at the same time? What loyalty will claim us when our various loyalties conflict with each other? What persons shall we acknowledge as neighbors and brothers under the covenant bonds of responsibility? Our answers to these questions do more than reveal what we are going to do. They declare who we are, what we think is important, how we view reality, where we stand, and who we are to be. Such declarations are fundamentally matters of faith, and they establish the inevitable links between faith and politics.

Foreign policy decisions are moral decisions and decisions in faith (in the sense which we have specified) for anyone, and not just for those who confess a particular faith. However, this book was written with a particular readership in mind: namely, the community of those who remember Jesus Christ, experience his presence, and hope for his coming in power and glory. We are concerned to ask, therefore, how Christians should think *as Christians* and what they should do *as Christians* with regard to the disposition of American power in international politics.

The first chapter attempts to establish the relationship between Christian faith and foreign policy, after a brief introduction to the policy process itself. Chapter 2 shows why moral considerations are pertinent to (indeed, binding on) the actions of states, and Chapter 3 points to the need for sensitivity to the impact of policy decisions and actions on the rights and interests of others.

In Chapter 4 we use the specific case of the American incursion into Cambodia in 1970 to set forth the criteria or standards statesmen should use as they seek to make moral decisions amid the conflicts of rights and duties. Chapter 5 is an attempt to think about the practicalities and the justice of using our own military forces to help other societies resolve their internal problems. Chapter 6 focuses the Christian ministry of reconciliation on what may be its hardest test: the relevance of reconciliation to the conflict between the U.S. and Communist countries. Chapter 7 speaks to the question of truthfulness in public statements about the conduct of the nation's foreign relations, and the final chapter cites some of the principal contributions Christian faith can make to the process of moral inquiry in foreign policy questions.

In no sense does this book cover the whole range of issues that confront the nation as it interacts with its political environment. We have mentioned economic questions only in passing. Were the book of greater length, we would have explored in some detail the highly important matters of international development, foreign investment policies, tariffs and trade relationships, and multilateral economic cooperation. Also, we would have given more extensive attention to international organization. But the book is more concerned about the *method* of decision-making and its supporting assumptions than about the substance of particular issues. The shape and focus of conflict will change across the years—at times with alarming suddenness—but the method of thinking about moral decision in foreign policy will remain constant.

CONTENTS

1 | Foreign Policy and Christian Faith

A Matter of Environmental Control

Foreign policy is the varied activity of states swimming in the sea of international society—trying to stay afloat, striking for speed or pacing for distance, enjoying the water, exercising tough or flabby muscles, competing with other swimmers, diving for treasure, evading the sharks. Whatever else a swimmer may do, he must see to his survival in the water. In order to do that—and therefore to be able to do other things—he must use his strength and wits and training to control his relationship to his watery environment.

So it is also with the conduct of foreign policy. Foreign policy is an activity of *states*—of those political institutions that are not legally subject to any higher government and that exist to promote the peace, order, justice, and general welfare of the peoples and territories under their jurisdiction. It is an activity in which they attempt to control and guide their relationships to their environment, or more specifically, to their *political* environment, which is composed primarily of other states. The purpose of the activity is the protection or promotion of anything that seems to have some significant bearing on the welfare of the state, its territory, and its people. Whatever a state may seek to safeguard or advance in this interaction with the political environment is called an *interest*. Those interests that relate directly to the survival of the state are called *vital interests*.

In the attempt to manage the interaction, states may use diplomatic negotiations, economic leverage, alliance with other states, and propaganda techniques (Voice of America and Radio Free Europe from one side, English-language broadcasts from Prague and East Berlin on the other)—or they may use the threat or direct application of military force. The common denominator of all these methods is *power*. The relationships of states with their political environments are power relationships *at least*.

To sum up: foreign policy is that activity of states whereby they use their power to guide and control their interaction with their political environment for the sake of their own interests. The total process of interaction among states is called *international politics*.

Who Initiates, Who Decides?

The U.S. Constitution assigns responsibility for foreign policy to Congress and the President, but it does not make clear just which branch has the authority to initiate and define policies. Presumably the executive branch is to *conduct* foreign policy, but who mainly is to *formulate* it?

Historically the initiative has been largely with the executive branch. That is partly because the conduct and the formulation of foreign policy cannot easily be separated, and partly because the President can move more directly and definitely to deal with crises in foreign relations than can the Congress. In our century, with the emergence of the United States as the preeminent world power in a time of enormous developments in communications and weapons, the movement of initiative and decision to the executive branch has been greatly increased. Very likely it will remain there.

Recently some members of Congress, especially in the Senate, have begun to rebel against that development and to insist on a more influential foreign policy role for Congress. There may be some redressing of the imbalance, but Congress probably will remain essentially in a criticizing and consenting role. In the absence of clear constitutional assignments of responsibility, practical considerations almost certainly will keep the initiative and the major powers of decision in the executive branch.

But who within the executive branch initiates and decides? President Harry S. Truman's favorite motto was "The buck stops here." When everyone else in the government has passed the buck, the President ultimately must take the blame for what goes wrong. Perhaps that is true, perhaps not. Some presidents have been known to "pass the buck"—to the news media, to the political opposition, to demonstrators in the streets, or to Congress. But even if it is true that the President is ultimately responsible, it does not mean that he is necessarily the prime mover in foreign policy, or even that he controls everything that is decided and done.

Two items will illustrate the point. First, Secretary of State John Foster Dulles literally dictated policy to President Eisenhower. Strong individuals not directly responsible to the people can emerge at any point in any administration and provide the initiative and decisiveness that chart the country's course. Second, the President and other top-level officials are dependent on the massive bureaucracy of the executive branch, not only for expert advice, but also for the clarification of alternatives. The men at the top usually decide on the basis of choices described to them by the men farther down the line. Often the most innovative, creative proposals are thrown out before they ever get to those who are supposed to be the decision-makers. Who then are the "deciders"?

In short, we cannot be sure who actually has the effective power of initiation and decision. If we find that unsettling, as we should, we should recognize the importance this adds to the discussion of moral responsibility for choices in foreign policy. Significant choice is not limited, practically speaking, to the President and the Secretary of State. It may become the opportunity of anyone who touches the policy process at any point.

The Limits of Choice

But can we really make significant choices, or are the alternatives so shaped by determining forces that they are not "alternatives" at all? According to one view, the events of the present are so strongly predisposed by events of the past that we may speak of them rightfully as "inevitable." Thus George F. Kennan, reviewing fifty years of American diplomatic history, saw the tragic course of affairs leading to World War II contained in the errors of the peace settlement of World War I.[1]

Others claim that basic considerations of geography determine the interests for which a nation must contend with its power. This view is called "geopolitics." Still others insist that economic interests control foreign policy decisions, not only by motivating choices, but also by providing the perspectives and biases that determine how the choices will be understood and evaluated.

We should take these and other arguments about limits and "realities" very seriously. The choices and possibilities of United States action in international politics are a good deal more limited than either the softhearted humanitarian or the hard-nosed anti-Communist realizes.

3

The United States cannot merely walk away from the worldwide involvements of its power, nor can it "roll back the iron curtain" with a resolute act of will. Nonetheless, these limits are not absolute. They are conditioning factors which restrict choice, but they do not eliminate choice.

We observe, for example, that first-term presidents tend to assume that it is important to the country that they be reelected in order to carry out their policies. So what do they do? As some persons see it, they design and adopt policies whose main reason for being is to promote their chances of reelection! Noting that development, we are inclined to say, "They ought not do that," which implies that they could have done otherwise. And they could have.

We are also aware that many persons outside the government attempt to influence the course of the nation's foreign policy. Some of them, such as defense contractors of foreign investors, do it for reasons of economic self-interest. Some advance the claims of other countries, such as Israel or the Arab states, with which the United States is involved politically. Others—including a large number of religious groups—advocate such policies as international development, disarmament, or international cooperation, based on "moral" considerations. Would any of them make the effort to influence policy decisions if there were no real choice?

But Is It Our Business?

There are indeed real limits to choice in foreign policy. But there are real choices, also, and the magnitude and implications of those choices make foreign policy vitally important business. The lives and fortunes of whole societies or, in an age of nuclear warheads, of all the world, sometimes ride on the formulation and execution of particular policies.

Not only is foreign policy important business—it is *our* business, and it is *my* business. According to the Constitution of the United States, the leaders of the country do not exercise power on their own behalf but on behalf of the people, including you and me. What they do with the power affects us in some very important ways. Their foreign policy decisions bring the threat of war closer or shove it away. They raise or lower (usually raise!) our taxes and the costs of goods and services. They alter the priority given those things we should be doing at home to serve the needs of our own people. They determine whether our sons will be commanded to put on uniforms and learn how to kill and perhaps risk being killed. I am not the President or the Secretary of State, but I am not poking my nose into someone else's affairs when I raise serious and sometimes highly critical questions about the practical and moral judgments in the planning and execution of the country's foreign policy. It is *my* business—my business as a man, a citizen, a taxpayer, a father. And for the very same reasons it is *your* business.

But right at that point we encounter a serious difficulty. This book is written to be read primarily (not exclusively, we hope) by Christian believers in the Christian community. That being the case, we must approach the matter of foreign policy responsibility with our Christian faith and commitment as the starting point. When we do that, we discover a sense of identity and an orientation to life that seem to be directly at odds with the aims and methods of foreign policy.

To see what the problem is, let us take a text from Paul: "Therefore, if any one is in Christ, he is a new cre-

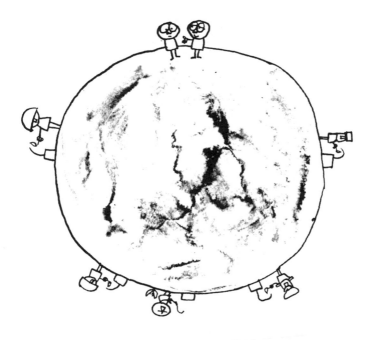

The Bomb used to bother me,
but I got used to it.

ation; the old has passed away, behold, the new has come."
(2 Cor. 5:17) The coming of Christ into human existence
poses a stark contrast between the old world and the new
world (cf. Eph. 2:1–10; Col. 3:1–17, etc.). When one
becomes a Christian, he enters the battle between the old
world and the new on the side of the new. His decision
means that he is a new creation—new from the center
of his being—and a citizen of God's new order. He puts
away his faith in the old gods and lives the Christian
faith, the life of new creatures in the new world.

Doesn't that mean he must put away any interest,
and certainly any direct involvement, in the process of
foreign policy and regard it firmly as none of his business
as a Christian? The new world of faith, we rejoice to confess, is marked by love, mercy, forgiveness, trust, openness, humility, self-sacrifice, and hope. Foreign policy,
by contrast, is marked by self-interest, power, manipula-
tion, deceit, seizure of advantage, defensiveness, distrust,
cynicism, pessimism, and the destruction of life and property. How can we be citizens of the new world and yet
act according to the ways of the old? How can we en-
gage in an activity whose very definition reveals it to be
an egoistic power process—a process in which the interests of one people are set in importance above those of
all other peoples in the world and pursued with the most
destructive means of coercion? What does that have to
do with the sacrificial love and the work of reconciliation
that are the very heart of the Christian faith?

On the other hand, if foreign policy is none of our
business *as Christians*, how can it be our business as men,
citizens, taxpayers, parents—unless we have found some
way to divide our persons so that "being a Christian" has
nothing to do with our lives as functioning human beings?

Some persons, unfortunately, resolve the conflict in

just that way. They park their Christian commitment in an area marked "Reserved for Spiritual Matters," and then take the commuter bus into the real world. Christianity for them is church and Sunday school and heaven and grace before meals, but not decisions about investments or hiring practices or candidates or bond elections. They believe in God and the hereafter, but they don't see that their belief has implications for man and the here-and-now.

Others don't see what the fuss is all about. As far as they are concerned, their country is on God's side—or vice versa—and whatever the country must do in its foreign contacts is done on behalf of God and righteousness. There is no tension between the new and the old worlds in their thought and action, only opposition between the good guys (us) and the bad guys (them).

There are yet others who feel so acutely the clash between political realities and Christian faith and love, that they attempt to make a clean break with political involvement. Politics is important, they concede, because a sinful world needs constraint and forceful guidance, but politics is not their work. Therefore they reject not only military service but also office-holding (for themselves) and sometimes even registering to vote. The world of time and history is divided between the old and the new: politics is old, Christ is new. But their lives are not divided; they are unified under the command of Christ. So they turn away from politics in order to witness to the coming kingdom of love and truth.

Here, then, are three ways of resolving the conflict between faith and politics: compartmentalization (faith is irrelevant to politics), alliance (God and country are partners), and radical separation (politics is incompatible with the life of faith).

Of the three options, only the third deserves our

respect, because it is the only one that takes seriously the sovereignty of God over all of life, the judgment of God on all human works, and the grace of God for all human need. But we cannot be satisfied with it. We cannot believe that a human enterprise in which the stakes are so high and the failures potentially so disastrous is of no vital concern to persons who are called to live out their lives in solemn awareness of the judgment of God and in joyous experience and anticipation of his redemptive power. Therefore we must probe further in our effort to grasp the relationships of Christian faith to foreign policy.

What Does the Bible Say?

If the Old Testament were the final authority for Christians, we could establish without difficulty the principle that the man of faith may—and in some cases must —make foreign policy his business. In the Old Testament we find the concept of the "holy war" set forth in Deuteronomy (chap. 20), Joshua (chaps. 6, 8, 10, 11), Judges (chaps. 1, 3—8, 20, and 21), and several other books. Amos prophesied not only against Israel, but against other nations as well. Jeremiah not only warned the rulers of Israel against putting their trust in alliances and armaments, but even advised King Zedekiah to surrender to the princes of the king of Babylon (Jer. 38:17–18). In the later parts of the Old Testament we often find prophecies of the victory of Israel over its national enemies under the leadership of Yahweh's Messiah.

But when a Christian reads the Old Testament he must read it in the light of the new covenant given in Jesus Christ. It is—or ought to be—immediately clear to him that he can have nothing to do with the "holy war" concept and its commands to destroy every living thing in the enemy's territories. Nor can he think at all in terms of the conflicts of Israel with its political opponents, for he is a member of the "new Israel," the church, which draws its membership from all the peoples of the earth. However, in the New Testament he finds no direct command or explicit calling to involve himself in questions of international politics. He is to "be subject to the governing authorities" (Rom. 13:1) and to "Honor the emperor." (1 Peter 2:17) There are limits to his subjection, to be sure, for he is to "obey God rather than men" (Acts 5:29) and to refuse to worship the state whenever it begins to make the claims that only God rightly can make (Rev. 13). But beyond those provisions he seems to be called on to wait for the final inbreak of the kingdom of God and not to concern himself with the business of the kingdoms of this world.

Score one for those who turn away from foreign policy on the grounds that it is no concern of Christ's new creations in the new world! But the game is not yet over. Often it is pointed out that the apathy of the New Testament toward Christian political responsibility was induced by the conviction that God soon would make an end of history as man knows it, and with it of all man's institutions. Read Paul's discussion of social statuses and responsibilities in 1 Corinthians 7. At issue there is the Christian's attitude not toward the state but toward marriage. He is urging an attitude of studied detachment. Why? Because of "the impending distress." (vs. 26) Because "the form of this world is passing away." (vs. 31) But that is exactly the same framework in which he discusses subjection to the governing authorities in Romans 13 (see vss. 11–12).

Now where does that leave us? It leaves us with

what always—explicity or implicity—has been a central difficulty for Christian faith: the fact that after nineteen hundred years of waiting, the end still has not come in the form or manner in which the earliest Christians expected it. It leaves us at the point of deciding whether to forsake all worldly involvements, to toss aside the Christian faith as irrelevant to the real business of life, or to rethink the relationship of our Christian faith to our worldly responsibilities.

As for me, I cannot imagine that the power and love of God and the person and work of Jesus Christ are irrelevant to the most important forms of human existence. Therefore, I must rethink the relationship of faith to life— to buying and selling, marrying and giving in marriage, education, recreation, relationships among the races—and to foreign policy. I anticipate that the Scriptures will give me some help, even if they cannot give me direct, unmistakable guidance.

A New Look at the Old World

Let us begin the rethinking by taking a new look at the "old world," which is the world of (among other things) international politics. Clearly it has not "passed away" in any literal sense. We have not found that as a result of our becoming new creatures in Christ, all our relationships are now characterized by love and brotherhood and trust (even in the church!). The rough and threatening old world is very much with us. We live and work in it. We respond to the questions it puts to us. We feel the weight of its pressures. Its continuing reality is what puts us under the necessity of making "faith decisions" and "moral decisions."

What sense does it make, then, to say we are in the new world and not the old? Let us again hear Paul: "From now on, therefore, we regard no one from a human point of view." (2 Cor. 5:16) The experience of becoming "a new creation" (2 Cor. 5:17) is in one respect a matter of our way of viewing reality. Heretofore we have looked out on the universe of time and space and matter and humanity with a merely human point of view, that is, with vision focused and colored by the values and prejudices and hopes of our slice of history and our spot on earth, of our human communities and our roles and statuses. Now, as new beings, we see reality in the light of the divine will and work. The old has passed away—it has lost its power to shape our minds and thereby order our actions. The new has come—it unveils the truth of what God has done, of what he is doing, of what he promises.

But what new understanding of political reality and our relationship to it proceeds from our new perspective? *First,* we recognize the world of political affairs as God's world. It is the same self-regarding, man-killing, God-rejecting world that murdered the Lord of life, but it is beloved by God—so beloved, we confess and proclaim, that God gave his Son for its redemption. God sustains and judges and recreates the fallen world. It is his "theater of operations." He works in and through all of its structures and processes, all of its actors and events, to make it whole.

Clearly, therefore (but it is clear only from the standpoint of faith), politics is not outside the scope of divine activity. It is a context of divine activity—a place where God strives to bring his will to fruition against the willfulness of man. Once a Christian recognizes this to be the case, any attempt to escape from political responsibility must be understood as an attempt to escape from responsibility to God.

Second, we see that man's political existence is caught

in the struggle between the "old" and the "new." Man's life in political society is not *as such* an aspect of the old world that is passing away. Man is by *nature* a "political animal," as Aristotle rightly taught us. His political relationships could not "pass away" without man himself passing out of existence. The problem, rather, is that these relationships are under the power of the "old world." They are egoistic, defensive, exploitative, threatening. They cripple and distort the human possibilities of realizing the love and freedom for which God created man. However, the active presence of God in the political world challenges the power of the old and thus creates new possibilities. Therefore, political existence is thrust into a condition of tension between the power and promise of the old and the power and promise of the new. This tension is heightened whenever and wherever there is powerful witness by word and deed to the reality of God in the midst of the reality of the political world.

Third, if God works in the midst of political affairs, we must work where he works, or else we put ourselves in the curious fix of claiming to cooperate in God's ministry while avoiding one large area of his work and some persons to whom he ministers. Furthermore, the nature of our work must be the same as the divine work: the healing of a broken world. Paul has nicely summarized the nature and relationship of God's activity and our responding commission in the familiar words of the Letter already quoted: "All this is from God, who through Christ reconciled us to himself and gave us the ministry of reconciliation; that is, God was in Christ reconciling the world to himself, not counting their trespasses against them, and entrusting to us the message of reconciliation." (2 Cor-5:18–19)

Perhaps the central difficulty is that of seeing the

ministry and message of reconciliation in specifically political terms.[2] We can overcome that difficulty if we recognize that our witness to God's reconciliation in Jesus Christ is given authentically only in the midst of our human activity—including our political activity—and not from some point outside it. We deliver the message not only in word but also in deed, and both word and deed must contribute to the liberation and renewal of man in the specific encounters of his daily existence.

So we Christians vote and protest and legislate and govern and sometimes even—with great pain in our hearts —bear arms, but always under the discipline of a mission to shape a new community over the gulf of old hostility, to set men free from the insecurity and suspicion which they inspire in each other, to feed the hungry and clothe the naked and liberate the oppressed and bring justice to the poor of the earth. It is a mission to demonstrate and realize, right in the midst of the old world, the power and love of God's new world which we have seen and known in Jesus Christ.

A Word About Offices

Some Christian traditions take politics with full seriousness as a work of love in response to the need of the neighbor in a fallen world, but they divide responsibility according to offices. There are those whose office it is to rule and others whose office it is to obey. Those who rule (and they alone) have full authority to make governmental decisions, including those that determine the uses of national power in international affairs. Those who do not rule should carry out their commands, but they should not try to mix in or interfere with governmental affairs that are not properly their own office.

We think that the matter of "office" should be regarded very seriously. Those who hold public office should regard their duties not only as a public trust but as a trust from God. They should lay the solemn responsibility for the whole conduct of their offices daily upon their consciences. But we do not believe that political responsibility can be divided so neatly and exclusively between those who have it and those who don't. In a democratic society the people ultimately are the governors. It is impossible for any political affairs to be "none of their business." Seen from the faith perspective we have described, no Christian can be altogether "non-political" if God works in the political field and calls us to share his work.

Some Words of Warning

So foreign policy is the business of us Christians. But lest that conviction produce a new distortion in our view of and relationship to the political process, let us heed two words of warning. First, foreign policy remains foreign policy even when addressed from the perspective of God's new order. It remains the "activity of states whereby they use their power to guide and control their interaction with their political environment for the sake of their own interests." Our Christian moral judgments must be made with an awareness of this continuing reality and not on the assumption that states can respond to simple moral appeals to surrender their power and pursue the interests of others but not their own.

Second, "new creatures in Christ" are new only by reason of the grace of God, not by reason of their superior righteousness or performance. As Martin Luther observed, the Christian is simultaneously a just man (by grace) and a sinner. Every moment of his life, every thought of his mind, every act of his will stand under the judgment of God and depend on his mercy. He is in no position to pronounce moral condemnations on others while excusing himself.

If we rightly grasp the nature of reality and of our mission, and if we heed these warnings, we shall be able as Christians to contribute faithfully and wisely to the understanding and making of moral judgments in United States foreign policy.

QUESTIONS FOR THOUGHT AND DISCUSSION

1. What do you think are the three most crucial problems of United States foreign policy? Why do you regard these as most crucial?

2. What is there about foreign policy and Christian faith that makes it difficult for us to see a connecting relationship between them?

3. In what ways, if any, does our Christian faith make it impossible for us to employ any of the normal practices of foreign policy?

4. What difference, if any, does a Christian perspective on political reality make in our understanding of it?

5. What, if any, political responsibilities does the church as a corporate body have?

2 | National Power and Moral Responsibility

Are States Morally Accountable?

The effective power of decision and action in the international world is the power of particular states. To whom or what is that power responsible? If you observe the behavior of states over a period of time, even a short period, you probably will discover that they hold themselves answerable ultimately to no authority higher than themselves. They may, of course, adhere to international laws and agreements in most of their dealings with other states, but where their vital interests are at stake, they will set the law aside if need be and resolve the conflict by force of arms. Nor can they be *made* responsible to international law except by the power of other states, for there is no world government organization with power of its own adequate to enforce the law. Moreover, even when the states join international organizations they keep the final prerogatives of political sovereignty in their own hands.

To be sure, these states are not eternal entities. The nation-state as we know it developed in Europe over a period of several hundred years. It was not there from the beginning. It is possible—many would say desirable— that this form of political organization will pass out of existence and be replaced by some other. But for the present and the forseeable future, it is the one we have to contend with. The state conducts foreign policy. It uses its power to implement its policies. And in doing so, it

sees its responsibility primarily to itself, its people, and its interests.

If that were the final word on responsibility in international politics, there would be no "moral issues" to discuss and no "moral judgments" to make. No state can be subject to moral limits in the pursuit of its objectives if there are no grounds for moral obligation or accountability to other political societies and their members. There would be practical problems of calculation and priority and risk, but no problems of moral decision. States might find it advantageous to maintain the appearance of moral rectitude, but they would not have to worry about acting morally when it was not convenient to do so. But is a state's concern for its own interests the final word? Is there, after all, no significant relation between morality and international politics? That question certainly is fundamental to this entire enterprise, and we must find a working answer to it before we go on to discuss the process of moral reasoning.

"No Moral Limits!"

Some perspectives on politics deny flatly—or with comparatively minor qualifications—that international morality is binding on states in the conduct of their foreign relations. We shall give brief (and over-simplified) consideration to three of them in this section.

Ultra-nationalism

We are hanging an "ultra" on this perspective to indicate that it goes beyond the ordinary garden-variety of nationalism in the claims it makes on behalf of the nation or the state. The ordinary varieties express the efforts of groups to gain a sense of group identity, to learn to recognize and appreciate their own past, and sometimes to summon their collective power to deal with a foreign oppressor. The "ultra" variety is idolatrous: it worships the nation or state and regards its good as the final test of all good.

The ultra-nationalist cannot tolerate international morality as a limit or guide to the behavior of his state, for his state is the source and symbol of morality. It defines what is right by what it does. It cannot do wrong. It should not even join international organizations, for by doing so it runs the risk of contaminating its purity by association with inferiors. If it should join such an organization, the reason should be merely one of temporary political necessity, and the obligations of membership should not be taken seriously, even if the state has promised solemnly to fulfill them.

The political history of the twentieth century proves that this attitude is not as unreal as it looks on paper. Moreover—and we should not overlook this point—it is possible for someone to be highly critical of ultra-nationalism in theory and yet come dangerously close to embracing it in his practice.

Marxism

According to the classical Marxist view, a true socialist state is not bound to observe the canons of international morality. That morality is not what it pretends to be—a neutral device for calling all states and peoples to a recognition of their responsibility to each other. Rather, it is a propaganda instrument the capitalist class has fabricated to tame the workers and peasants. They are to be persuaded by so-called moral teaching that it is their duty to accept the exploitation to which they are subjected, and that they will be guilty of grave immorality if they rise up against their oppressors. Meanwhile capitalist states themselves do not adhere to the rules and requirements of the morality they propagate; they follow their class interests.

As the Marxist sees it, authentic moral relationships are possible only in a classless society, where human beings are not alienated from each other and from their work by the private ownership of the means of production. The revolution will prepare the conditions for the emergence of the classless society. In the meantime, what is morally right is what serves the cause of the revolution.

In practice, Marxist states sometimes accommodate themselves in limited ways to the "bourgeois morality" they reject in theory. That happens when they find it necessary or to their advantage to cooperate with their ideological opponents. It happens also when they discover that socialist states can have serious differences among themselves over questions of national interest.

Political Realism

Political realism discounts the moral responsibility of states because international politics, according to its view, is a power process and not a moral process. It is a process in which states seek to maximize their power in support of their interests, and they are limited not by moral scruples but by the power of other states doing the same thing. The political realist is not an ultra-nationalist: he does not believe that his state is God. But he does believe that it is a state, and that it must operate according to the power principles that govern the behavior of states, and not the moral principles that govern the behavior of individual persons.[1]

Moral principle is not merely irrelevant to foreign policy; it is positively dangerous, because it introduces an alien element into the calculations of interest and power. Ambassador George F. Kennan, to whom we referred in the first chapter, argued forcefully in his *American Diplomacy, 1900–1950,* that some of the most serious mistakes in U.S. foreign policy were caused by attempts to direct policy according to moral principle rather than according to national interest.[2]

"There Are Moral Limits!"

As children of Western civilization we are heirs to philosophical and religious traditions that universalize moral responsibility and affirm the personhood and rights of every human being—the stranger as well as the friend and brother. So long as these traditions hold some power over our minds, we cannot concede that states have no responsibilities beyond their own interests. In this section we shall consider the implications of two of these traditions, Stoicism and Christianity.

Stoicism

Stoicism, one of the great philosophies of Greece and Rome, many themes of which are held by contemporary humanists, identifies man's reason as the foundation of universal morality. Each human being is a rational being; therefore he should be free of domination by others. All human beings are rational beings; therefore they are fundamentally equal, and there is no natural distinction between masters and slaves. Every human being possesses his rationality as a "spark" of the one divine reason; therefore all are brothers. Liberty, equality, brotherhood: these principles of a universal morality challenge every effort and temptation to confine moral responsibility to the members of a single group.

Christianity

In its attitude toward the scope of moral responsibility, Christianity disregards and even negates the preferences and groupings to which man assigns so much importance. Its sharp contrast with merely human views of morality is set forth in the following well-known passage: "You have heard it was said, 'You shall love your neighbor and hate your enemy.' But I say to you, Love your enemies and pray for those who persecute you, so that you may be sons of your Father who is in heaven; for he makes his sun rise on the evil and on the good, and sends rain on the just and on the unjust." (Matt. 5:43–45)

The ordinary expectation is that we are to love neighbors and hate enemies—nothing more radical than that. But if we are to be sons of our Father in heaven, something quite different is expected—we are to love the enemy! So obviously the normal behavior of states is not the final word. Hatred of the enemy may be the usual response of peoples involved in international conflict, but it is not a rightful—and certainly not a praiseworthy—response.

Moreover, even the neighbor—as Jesus defined him (Luke 10:29–37)—is not the neighbor we recognize in ordinary human concepts of responsibility. He is not primarily the friend or kinsman or fellow countryman. He is the person who needs our help—any person, anywhere in the world, of any race. The impoverished countries, the "underdeveloped" countries, the countries living under foreign domination or left-wing or right-wing dictatorships, all are our "neighbors" in the Christian meaning of the term. And when we show compassion on them and put ourselves at their disposal, we (by the grace of God) are their neighbors.

"By the grace of God." That, of course, explains the breadth and inclusiveness of our responsibility, as well as the power to love the enemy and to serve the needs of strange or unknown neighbors. "With men this is impossible, but with God all things are possible." (Matt. 19:26) The human possibilities of love are transformed. God reconciled us to himself even while we regarded him as our enemy (Rom. 5:10). By the same grace he has reconciled us to our human enemies in Jesus Christ and made it possible for us to love them as brothers for whom Jesus Christ also died.

Thus the human inclination to serve only those who in some way serve us is transformed by the divine grace bestowed on the evil and on the good, on the just and on the unjust. God does not help only "those who help themselves." He helps the helpless. And what is even more offensive to our merely human views of responsibility, he helps also those who *will not* help themselves.

According to the Christian confession, therefore, the self-interest of states is not the final word on political responsibility. God has established a field of moral relationships as wide and as long as the whole of humankind.

False Solutions

If we want a working answer to the question of political responsibility, we cannot grab it out of the air or write it up as a neat formula. Why not? Because we are historical beings, not free-floating minds, and our working definitions and guidelines have to make some sense in terms of what we remember and experience and hope for.

In the history we know, two elements interact with each other to create the problem of "morality and politics." One element is the continuing power over thought and conscience (if not action) of the traditions of universal moral responsibility. The other element is the reality of political organization in the form of legally sovereign states. Neither element can be simply wiped from our memories or our experience. Therefore we cannot project a future that does not account for both of them. Any attempt to do so is a false solution.

It is a false solution if in pursuit of political moralism we urge the various states to forsake interest and power in obedience to higher principle and wider responsibility. "If only states would trust each other," we complain. However, the plain fact is that states trust each other only when they have no conflicts of interest and when the history of their association has created some basis for confidence. When there is a serious conflict of interest, and when there is no such reassuring history, the states will not substitute simple trust for minimum security guarantees.

Moreover, we should learn to appreciate the fact that statesmen often pursue the national interests of their countries out of a sense of moral responsibility, and not merely as a cynical grab for power. They see their office as a trusteeship. If they surrender what they believe to be the justifiable interests of their country, they are betraying the trust of office. We have misconstrued the clash between national interests and wider definitions of responsibility as a clash of "politics" with "morality." Often it is a conflict between two definitions of moral responsibility. We do not grasp the acuteness of the moral crisis in foreign policy until we see the matter in these terms.[3]

On the other hand, it is a false solution if we attempt to discount or repress the traditions of universal moral responsibility. Their truth is part of our way of thinking, and we cannot shove them out of our minds or down into the subconscious without doing violence to our manner of understanding and relating to reality. The result of such attempts often is political fanaticism.

Correlating Conflicting Responsibilities

There is no way out of it. If we are going to describe and speak to the moral requirements of national power, we must reckon with the fact that states are situated in two lines of moral responsibility. They are bound to discharge their responsibilities to that segment of humanity that is specifically under their jurisdiction. But in doing so, they are not justified in acting as laws unto themselves. They must acknowledge and honor as just limits and justifiable claims the rights and needs of other persons and groups in international society.

On some occasions these two lines of responsibility happily will converge. We do in fact live in an interdependent world, and there is a good deal of correlation or reciprocity between what we need as a nation and what the world needs as a habitable dwelling for us all. On other occasions the lines diverge or intersect, and it becomes necessary to make a hard choice between what is necessary and justifiable to us as a national society and what we owe to others or what is good for the world as a whole. Those are the most serious, most difficult occasions for moral judgment.

We can expect—on the basis of what we have learned of international politics—that when states are confronted with such decisions they will look first to their own interests. Therefore it is hardly necessary for Christians and other persons of moral sensitivity to urge them to do so. It is much more fitting for us to throw whatever weight we have on the other side, and to keep pressing the states—especially our own—to remember and respect those other obligations.

But we must speak *to* their national responsibilities and not simply *against* them. And that means we should encourage them to build into their foreign policy processes some constant assumptions about and criteria for dealing justly with the rights and claims of others. For one thing, they should expand their *awareness of the human reality* of other persons and peoples caught up in the political process, and of the impact on them of decisions and actions which support the national interest. For another, they should submit to the discipline of *justifying their decisions* and giving reasons for their actions when their policies run counter to the just expectations of others. These two points are the subject matter of the next two chapters.

Ultimately, however, the real test of a moral decision is whether it intends to create lines of communication and fabric of community to bridge the gap between opponents in international politics. That intention is a clear political expression of the Christian mission of reconciliation. The significance of that intention is a premise of every chapter, not just of one in particular.

QUESTIONS FOR THOUGHT AND DISCUSSION

1. What evidence, if any, of "ultra-nationalism" do you see in American attitudes toward national interest and relationships with other countries?

2. What truth, if any, is there in the Marxist charges that "capitalist" states do not themselves adhere to the moral standards that they use to condemn the behavior of "Communist" states?

3. What possible harm could it do for statesmen to conduct foreign policy on a basis of moral principle rather than with reference to national interest and power?

4. Does Jesus' admonition to love the enemy have any realistic bearing on the conflicts of international politics? Why or why not?

5. Some years ago the United States Congress authorized a huge shipment of grain to India to relieve a major famine, but only on the condition that India not sell strategic war materials to Communist countries. Should we insist that aid given to relieve human suffering serve our national interest, or should we disregard considerations of national interest in such cases?

3 | A Humanly Sensitive Foreign Policy

Two Types of Sensitivity

When states pursue their interests in international politics, they do not glide through vast open space like astronauts on their way to the moon. Rather, they touch something solid wherever they reach, and the things they touch are the rights and interests of other peoples and states. Foreign policy set in motion is bound to move something that belongs to someone else. A plunge into the sea of international politics (or international economics) may produce a tidal wave on the opposite shore.

But do states actually look around or look ahead to see who might be drenched or drowned by the waves they make? If their policy-making elites are at all competent, they will do so. A prudent statesman knows he can defeat his own plans if he provokes unexpected and forceful reactions. But he is not necessarily dissuaded from his plans by the realization that someone "out there"—even an "innocent bystander"—surely will be hurt if he moves ahead. The prudent statesman may have cultivated a high degree of sensitivity to the views and feelings and interests of other states and peoples only because it is smart politics to know in advance where the opposition will come from and how serious it will be. He may pursue a significant advantage even though his power moves send a destroying flood across the fabric and flesh of other societies.

Given the perspective on politics that we have established in this book, "smart politics" ought not to provide the primary motivation—and certainly not the exclusive motivation—for political sensitivity. Political elites ought to be acutely sensitive to the near- and far-ranging effects of their policies, but the foundation of their concern should be their awareness of what human beings owe to other human beings by reason of their common humanity. Questions of gain and loss should be interpreted and controlled with reference to that awareness.

We are talking about the type of sensitivity that encourages a morally serious foreign policy, and not just about the type that makes for a skillful foreign policy. Certainly we intend to underscore the need for wisdom and skill, but everyone intends to do that. Our peculiar task is to stress those dimensions of political responsibility that otherwise might be shoved aside. Most states use moral rhetoric—sometimes a great deal of it—in making public explanations of their policies. What we want to know is whether there is hard evidence of moral seriousness.

The first and most reliable evidence comes in answer to the question, "Do states and policy-makers really care about the human impact of their policies?" That is, do they care for reasons that pertain to the rights and welfare of those affected, and not because it's "smart politics"? Is there genuine sensitivity to culture, feelings, pain, and hopes, as well as to geography and treasure, or only astute awareness of numbers and obstacles? Is the sensitivity self-conscious, deliberate, and sustained? Does it apply to a regular review of current policies as well as to the development of future ones? Is there visible evidence that it exerts significant influence on the shaping, revising, or canceling of policies? Is there real moral commitment, or only the shrewdness of the sharp and cynical operator?[1]

We intend to direct these questions to the conduct

of United States foreign policy, but before we get to that point, let us record an item of agreement between the concerns for political effectiveness and for moral seriousness. A policy process that characteristically disregards or is blind to the human effects of its decisions and actions is geared to failure politically as well as morally. It will be politically incompetent at the very moment real competence is needed to avert major disaster. It will be morally arrogant and irresponsible in the crises that plead for compassion and responsibility. And a society that breeds such insensitivity into the attitudes of its own people and its political elites will fail to fulfill the demands of its historical vocation.

Therefore, every state needs a self-study of the "sensitivity factor" built into its policy process as an integral, constant, and rigorous element. And in view of the fact that awareness and insensitivity are socially-derived attitudes, the self-study process needs to be turned also against the society itself.

A Good Example of Bad Diplomacy

Earlier we made reference to George F. Kennan. In *Memoirs 1925–1950,* Ambassador Kennan records a striking example of unqualified insensitivity in the conduct of foreign relations.[2] It occurred during World War II, when Kennan, not yet an ambassador, was placed in temporary charge of the United States legation in Lisbon. Portugal had not entered the war on either side, but it did have a historic alliance with Great Britain. The British decided to invoke the alliance to request permission to construct military bases in the Azores Islands, which belonged to Portugal. The Portuguese, although officially neutral and fully mindful of the serious risk of reprisals from the Germans, agreed to honor the alliance and grant the request.

At the same time the United States Department of War (which, according to Kennan, had imperiously wrested the conduct of foreign affairs from the timid State Department) decided that the United States also needed bases in the Azores to facilitate the movement of aircraft and supplies to England. However, American "diplomatic negotiations" with the Portuguese were markedly different from those of the British, who had been scrupulously correct and respectful in every detail and had used great caution to minimize the risk of German retaliation against Portugal.

In the first place, the high officials in Washington who called the tune apparently regarded Prime Minister Salazar of Portugal as a minor nuisance who should be accorded the diplomatic deference due to someone of the international stature of, for example, the mayor of Flowery Branch, Georgia. Kennan reports that there had never been a political discussion between the American ambassador and Salazar at any time since the entry of the United States into the war. Assurances of United States respect for Portuguese neutrality should have been given as a matter of course. They were not. When the decision finally was made to offer the assurances, "Washington" instructed Kennan to arrange an interview with Dr. Salazar, and then cabled him again only minutes before the interview was to begin, ordering him not to discuss the matter of the neutrality guarantees!

In the second place, American "requests" to Portugal were in reality demands. The guarantees of neutrality, it turned out, were withheld as a bargaining chip. What would the United States offer Portugal in return for concessions in the Azores? The United States would offer to respect

Portuguese neutrality! The implication was clear: if Portugal did not honor the "requests," the United States would take what it wanted anyway.

In the third place, the American demands (correction: "requests") were of typically American gargantuan proportions. They dwarfed what the British—even with their age-old and hallowed alliance—had dared to ask. The United States wanted bases of several kinds, port facilities, shore accommodations, radar installations, and numerous other wartime "necessities." No consideration had been given to the effect of this enormous American "presence" on the Azores. Kennan writes:

> It was perfectly clear that facilities of these dimensions would simply sink the economy and administration of the islands under their own weight. The Portuguese share in what went on in the islands would, in the face of such an establishment, necessarily be reduced to secondary dimensions. The primitive economy of the islands would be debauched by the amount of outside money brought in and expended. The islanders themselves, heretofore self-respecting people, would inevitably be moved to abandon their humble farms and other pursuits and to embrace, for the superior remuneration involved, the status of servicing personnel for the bases. It was idle to pretend that this represented anything other than a virtual takeover of the islands by our armed forces for the duration of the war and the ruination of the culture and traditional mode of life of the inhabitants.[3]

The moral irresponsibility of this exercise in political insensitivity is fully evident. Policy-makers at the highest level treated the leader of another sovereign state—

neutral but friendly—in a manner that surely must have been regarded as a personal affront. They also proposed in effect to occupy part of his country's territory and to assume the dominant role in determining its present and future. They laid out grandiose plans for "improvements" on the real estate, with no thought for the disruption of culture, economy, identity, and moral discipline that the implementation of their plans would entail. They subjected a small country to unnecessary and unacceptable risks of reprisal by a hostile and vindictive power. And all of this was done with no apparent awareness or even concern that they were doing anything that might be open to question as to its moral responsibility!

The political incompetence of the maneuver is hidden somewhat by the fact that really serious complications were muted or avoided, partly through luck and partly through the courage and insight of a few individuals. But the penalties for insensitive blundering were always near at hand. Had the United States directly violated Portuguese neutrality, the action very likely would have provoked nervously neutral Spain to enter the war on the side of the Axis powers. Moreover, it might even have forced Portugal to invoke the Anglo-Portuguese Alliance in its own defense. As Portugal had honored the alliance to support England, now England would be asked to honor it to support Portugal by defending Portugal against England's primary wartime ally, the United States!

However, in a case like this, one should not attempt to distinguish political incompetence from moral irresponsibility. Each is an aspect of the other; both are the result of galloping insensitivity to the human reality of other people who happen to be caught up in the historical execution of our own policies.

But Is It Characteristic?

We would like to believe that this clear example of barbarous insensitivity was merely an isolated incident generated by the impatience of harried and fatigued men striving desperately to win a war that was destroying much of Europe. There is no doubt that the pressures of the wartime situation had much to do with it, but unfortunately the attitudes of the decision-makers represent a constant and characteristic element in the style of United States foreign policy. We have a strong inclination to be heavy-handed, shortsighted, paternalistic, and a little deaf in our foreign relations. That is not the whole picture, but if we painted those elements out of the picture we would not be recognized in what remained. There is just too much evidence—from our relations with allies and with Latin America, from our intervention practices, from our economic expansionism, from our attitude toward revolutions against repressive regimes—for us to set the charge aside.

Why is this tendency "characteristic"? In the first place, it is a characteristic of the powerful, and not of the United States alone. Any person or state or corporation that possesses and disposes of great power is tempted to look on persons or groups of lesser power as part of the environment to be manipulated or ignored. King David's involvement with Bathsheba (2 Samuel 11—12) was not just the action of a man tempted to commit adultery; it was also the action of a man of great power accustomed to taking what he wanted and not worrying about the violated rights and feelings of his victims. His particular sin was the fruit of his lust. His attitude was the fruit of his position of unrivaled dominance.

And the LORD sent Nathan to David. He came to him, and said to him, "There were two men in a certain city, the one rich and the other poor. The rich man had very many flocks and herds; but the poor man had nothing but one little ewe lamb, which he had bought. . . . Now there came a traveler to the rich man, and he was unwilling to take one of his own flock or herd to prepare for the wayfarer who had come to him, but he took the poor man's lamb, and prepared it for the man who had come to him." Then David's anger was greatly kindled against the man; and he said to Nathan, "As the LORD lives, the man who has done this deserves to die; and he shall restore the lamb fourfold, because he did this thing, and because he had no pity."

Nathan said to David, "You are the man."

(2 Samuel 12:1–7)

Many of the people of Latin America seem to feel that there is something of King David in the attitude the *yanquis* have taken toward them across the generations. The United States has been the self-appointed guardian of the hemisphere, but as "guardian" it has looked mainly to its own interests, has taken from Latin America what it wanted, and has paid little heed to the impact of its actions on those countries and their peoples. The "Good Neighbor Policy" toward Latin America was devised to assure the friendship and loyalty of those countries during World War II. The "Alliance for Progress" was initiated by President John Kennedy to keep Latin America from "going Communist." But there is little evidence that we have tuned our ears to hear the *latinos* speak of their interests in their own terms.

A second reason why the insensitivity is characteristic is more specifically American. We are not, as a people, much interested in such things as the careful manicuring of miniature Japanese gardens. But we are enthusiastic about (and really very good at) bulldozing mountains and forests and fine old residential areas in order to lay out our superhighways and shopping centers and apartment complexes. And we can get very short-tempered with someone who "resists progress" by filing suit to keep our bulldozers from destroying his home and neighborhood.

That presents problems for our behavior abroad as well as at home. Kennan's complaint about inattention to the probable effects of United States "occupation" of the Azores could very well have been written about our intervention in Vietnam. All the fears that he raised about economic dislocation, cultural disruption, and deterioration of moral discipline have been realized in our massive involvement in that country. Whatever justification there may or may not be in our reasons for intervening, it is clear that our "engineering" approach to the penetration of another society has created the impression of an elephant walking sentry duty in a watermelon patch.

A third reason also is peculiarly American: we know that we are doing what is right and good for other people, so how could we possibly be doing them any harm?

This analysis is bound to be unpopular, because no one likes to be criticized, and even less does he like to be told that his wrongdoing is a typical expression of his personality. But if one is inclined to turn away from the criticism and retreat into his wounded righteousness, he should remember Jesus' warning against "some who trusted in themselves that they were righteous." (Luke

18:9–14) It is extremely dangerous to put ourselves in a position of being unable to receive forgiveness by insisting that we have not sinned and therefore do not need to be forgiven. We shall endure much more loss and inflict much more suffering if we refuse to recognize in ourselves and in our practice what others surely know to be the case.

The Morally Sensitive Stance

What, then, should we do differently? How will a morally sensitive statesman plan foreign policy? At the outset, he will survey the whole field of action and identify the other peoples and states likely to be affected. Then he will attempt to stand where they stand and see what they see and think what they think, in order to imagine how the operation will strike them and how they

Your report indicates   Yes sir.   Don't they like   Yes sir, I think
civilian morale is low.   our chewing gum?   it's the napalm.

probably will respond. Moreover, he will use this method also for regular review of policies already in operation. Of course, he knows that international relations often come to a contest over rights and interests, and that in such contests he will be expected to advocate and support his country's side. But because he is a just man, and not merely a shrewd or prudent man, he will try to minimize the damage done to others in the pursuit of what he believes to be justifiable ends.

To have that kind of concern he must conquer the strong and persistent temptation to see humanity only in the features and dress of his own people. To maintain such concern, he must approach his work in a spirit of repentance—repentance for much harm already done and much that surely will be done even by the most careful (full of care) uses of power.

Mmm. Napalm has a nasty chemical sound to it.

Let's call it Freedom Fire!

If those are the requirements of a humanly sensitive foreign policy, and if foreign policy must be humanly sensitive to be both just and effective, then Christian faith and witness are equipped to make singular contributions to the policy process. For Christian faith holds the humanity of strangers and enemies ever before us, and Christian witness testifies to the judgment that must intervene before we can lay hold of the riches of divine grace.

QUESTIONS FOR THOUGHT AND DISCUSSION

1. What is the difference between being humanly sensitive and being politically alert in the conduct of foreign policy? Can an effective political decision-maker really afford to be *humanly* sensitive?

2. Do Americans tend to take an "engineering approach" to the solving of human problems? Give reasons for your answer. Does that approach make us less sensitive to the fullness and uniqueness of human life?

3. What is the relationship between technological advance and progress?

4. For years the U.S. Navy has used the island of Culebra as a target range, and now the island is becoming almost uninhabitable. How do you compare the values of the battle efficiency of the U.S. Navy, on one hand, and the desires, the way of life, and the culture of the Culebrans on the other?

5. Are you aware that American-owned firms have taken over a large share of European and Canadian industry? [4] How do you feel about this? Would you be uneasy about this trend if you were a European or a Canadian?

6. What resources of Christian faith can help increase the moral sensitivity of foreign policy?

4 | Giving Reasons for Our Violations

Just Purposes Versus Just Limits

What should a morally conscientious statesman do when he is pursuing what he believes to be rightful interests of his country, but discovers that he cannot continue to do so without violating the rights or harming the interests of some other country? Should he (1) always stop short of violation, or should he (2) always set the limits aside when his cause in his estimation is just? Or should he (3) reject both of these absolute rules and adopt a process of moral deliberation that tests policies in particular cases, in order to distinguish between just and unjust violations?

Certainly the third choice is the correct one. The first one begets injustice when it denies significant goals for the sake of avoiding comparatively insignificant violations. The second one threatens to make an idol of the national good and seek it alone in every encounter. The third choice, however, recognizes that violations sometimes are justifiable, but it denies that a just cause is always just grounds for violation. By using a checklist of questions to investigate situations of moral conflict, it can be determined whether a particular violation is justifiable.

The Moral Argument

A good example of the third approach was President Richard Nixon's speech on his decision to send United States forces into Cambodia on April 30, 1970.[1] The occasion for the action was a new threat to the safety of American troops and to American policy objectives, due to the fact that North Vietnam was increasing its military strength in Cambodia at the same time that the United States was withdrawing troops from South Vietnam. Mr. Nixon considered the several policy alternatives created by this situation and decided that the only reasonable course was to strike at the Communist sanctuaries in Cambodia.

His speech to the American people was more than merely a report on the developments. It was a moral argument.[2] He described the situation, clarified his responsibilities, reported the nature and extent of the action taken, and gave reasons to justify the decision. In this chapter we intend to identify and analyze the process of moral reasoning Mr. Nixon used to justify the violation of an established limit to the use of national power.

What issue required moral deliberation and justification? Obviously it was the prospective violation of Cambodian neutrality. The President's statement was set up to deal primarily with that question. American policy since 1954, he contended, "has been to scrupulously respect the neutrality of the Cambodian people." By contrast, North Vietnam for five years had built up sanctuaries in that country for hit-and-run attacks against the opposing forces in South Vietnam. "For five years, neither the United States nor South Vietnam has moved against those enemy sanctuaries because we did not wish to violate the territory of a neutral nation." He concluded, however, that it had become necessary for the U.S. to do what it had carefully and conscientiously avoided doing in the past, namely, send its troops across the Cambodian border to destroy the sanctuaries. How did he justify that admitted violation of generally accepted international law?

President Nixon used a set of moral criteria that are best known for their use in determining whether a resort to war is justifiable. He did not use them by name, as we shall do in our analysis, but there is no doubt that he was employing those categories. There must be a *just cause* for the action, and it must be limited by a *rightful intention*. Those who commit the state to war must have the *legitimate authority* to do so. The anticipated costs (in life and in property) must be in *proportion* to the significance of the cause and not exceed it. The course decided upon must be the *last resort,* and there must be a *reasonable hope of success.*

All of these criteria are aspects of a single process of moral reasoning. There must be a "just cause" before the inquiry can proceed further, but even a cause a considerable weight cannot justify a violation that fails the other moral tests.

Just Cause

Just cause for the violation might have been the correction of an injustice, namely, the illegal occupation of Cambodian territory by the North Vietnamese. But that was not the purpose of the American action. Rather, it was to repel an injury that, according to the President, almost certainly would occur if the buildup were allowed to proceed unchecked. The "injury" that was stressed at the beginning of Mr. Nixon's speech and remained the central motif throughout was the prospect of heavy casualties to American forces. "I have concluded," he said, "that the actions of the enemy in the last ten days clearly endanger the lives of Americans who are in Vietnam now and would constitute an unacceptable risk to those who will be there after withdrawal of another

150,000." In the structure of the moral argument, that injury was the primary reason for asserting "just cause."

But that was not the only prospective "injury" Mr. Nixon cited as just cause for attacking the sanctuaries in Cambodia. As the speech unfolded, threatened values were piled on top of threatened values, until it seemed that the future of the United States and of the "free world" required the decision.

1) The goals of the American intervention in Vietnam were threatened. Thus, the attack was not only "To protect our men who are in Vietnam," but also "to guarantee the continued success of our withdrawal and Vietnamization programs." The action would serve "the purpose of ending the war in Vietnam and winning the just peace we all desire."

2) Cambodian neutrality also—obviously—was threatened by the North Vietnamese. Although Mr. Nixon did not explain the move as an attempt to rescue Cambodia, he did state that the United States would provide aid "for the purpose of enabling Cambodia to defend its neutrality."

3) More broadly, the North Vietnamese buildup threatened the entire Pacific policy: "The possibility of winning a just peace in Vietnam and in the Pacific is at stake."

4) The prestige necessary to effective world leadership was being called into question. If the United States responded to this arrogant and aggressive threat "merely by plaintive diplomatic protests . . . the credibility of the United States would be destroyed in every area of the world where only the power of the United States deters aggression." Not "our power but our will and character . . . is being tested," and "If when the chips are down the

U.S. acts like a pitiful helpless giant, the forces of totalitarianism and anarchy will threaten free nations and free institutions throughout the world."

5) National pride was at stake, and the President said he was willing to put his political future on the line in order to protect the self-image of the United States as unconquered and preeminent in the world: "I would rather be a one-term President than to be a two-term President at the cost of seeing America become a second-rate power and to see this nation accept the first defeat in its proud 190-year history." He warned the North Vietnamese that ". . . we will not be humiliated. We will not be defeated."

Rightful Intention

The action that violates what in most circumstances is a just limit must intend nothing more than to correct the injustice or repel the injury and restore the conditions of just relationships. According to the traditional Christian formula, it should not seek vengeance against the opponent, for "Vengeance is mine, I will repay, says the Lord." (Rom. 12:19) Also, the responder to the unjust action should not use the occasion to gain benefits beyond what would constitute just payment for any loss.

On this point, Mr. Nixon was more careful than he had been in reciting the just causes. The attack on the sanctuaries was "not for territory—not for glory." "Our purpose is not to occupy the areas. Once enemy forces are driven out of these sanctuaries and once their military supplies destroyed, we will withdraw." American aid would help Cambodia defend its neutrality, but it was "not for the purpose of making it an active belligerent on one side or the other." Obviously signaling his intentions to China, he stated that "These actions are in no way directed at the security interests of any nation."

Legitimate Authority

"Legitimate authority" is the question of the right to exercise power. Did the President have the right to exercise the power of the nation? There is no disputing his authority to act as the chief foreign policy officer of the United States, but there were serious questions as to whether he might have exceeded his authority in this particular case. In his own view, the decision was a legitimate and necessary one for the commander in chief of the armed forces. Moreover, he sought to claim the authority of popular support for his decision by repeated insistence that a majority of the American people favored the ends that his action was designed to serve. That is not the same as saying that a majority of the people supported the action itself, but the President nonetheless presented his "majority" observation as evidence of authorization.

Aside from that, did the United States have the right to exercise power over others who were not subject to its legal jurisdiction, and who, in the case of Cambodia, were not even belligerents? In international conflict the right to exercise power over others is conferred ultimately by the *necessity* of using the particular means to serve a just cause. Mr. Nixon believed that he had demonstrated that necessity.

Moreover, he hinted at additional authorization by claiming that "Cambodia . . . has sent out a call to the United States, to a number of other nations, for assistance." That would make the border-crossing an instance of "intervention by invitation," and it would resolve the authority question satisfactorily. But although Cambodia had indeed requested aid, it had not directly asked for *troops*, and the Cambodian government apparently was surprised to learn of the movement of forces across its borders. Moreover, it was more than a little uneasy about the situation, because the Vietnamese—whether of the South or of the North—are traditional enemies of the Cambodians. Nevertheless, the Lon Nol government was in no position to repudiate the action, and its inability to do so lent some credence to the intimation of "intervention by invitation."

Proportion

The North Vietnamese buildup constituted an "unacceptable risk," which meant that the cost of sustaining the injury would be proportionately greater than the cost of repelling it. Were the means to be employed proportionate and appropriate to the offense? Yes. Massive aid to the Cambodian army would be inappropriate, because the army could not absorb and use it. And a mild diplomatic protest would fail to accomplish the end and would make matters worse by inviting further aggression. Firm and decisive military action aimed at destroying the sanctuaries was the only appropriate and proportionate response.

Last Resort

Had all other means been exhausted before proceeding with the violation? According to President Nixon, the United States had done everything possible to avoid encroaching on Cambodian sovereignty. First, it had tolerated the "privileged sanctuaries" for five years, during which time "we counseled patience to our South Vietnamese allies and imposed restraints on our own com-

manders." Second, he had not ordered retaliation at the
beginning of the buildup, but had issued a firm warning
that he "would not hestitate to take strong and effective
measures to deal with that situation" if he became con-
vinced that it posed a serious danger to the lives of
American servicemen left in South Vietnam after large-
scale withdrawal. Third, the United States had reduced
its operations in the theater of war and had pressed regularly and earnestly for a negotiated settlement, only to
be met by "intransigence at the conference table, belli-
gerence in Hanoi, massive military aggression in Laos and
Cambodia, and stepped-up attacks in South Vietnam designed to increase American casualties."

The Question of Coherence

The substance of President Nixon's moral argument
justifying the violation of Cambodian neutrality was that
it was counter-intervention responding to previous intervention by the North Vietnamese and seeking to prevent
additional unacceptable injury. He argued the case primarily by using the traditional criteria of the justice of
resort to war, although he did not call the criteria by
name. The one criterion not dealt with was that of "reasonable hope of success." Apparently the President never
doubted that the attack would succeed in its objectives.

The question we want to raise at this point is
whether Mr. Nixon offered a sound and coherent moral
argument. It is not easy to deal with such a question ob-
jectively, because there is little doubt that most of us
responded to the Cambodian decision on the basis of our
feelings about American intervention in Vietnam as such.
Presumably, most persons who supported the intervention
supported the incursion into Cambodia also. Quite obvi-

ously most, if not all of the persons who opposed the
intervention policy opposed the incursion as well. Nonetheless, we should be able to test out the publicly-presented
moral argument to see if it hangs together.

There can be no argument at all if the action was
not supported by a defensible cause. The action must also
pass the tests posed by the other criterio, but the question
of "just cause" is the fundamental one. At the beginning
of his speech, Mr. Nixon stated a "cause" that, taken by
itself, created a strong presumption for justification:
namely, the protection of American troops from suffering
massive casualties during the program of withdrawal. It
is hard to fault a commander for taking extraordinary
measures to protect his forces when they are withdrawing
from combat. But no sooner had the President set up this
supporting reason than he began to introduce a line of
additional "causes," such as protecting the Vietnamization
program, bringing the war to an end, securing U.S. policy
objectives in the Pacific, maintaining U.S. world prestige,
and avoiding "the first defeat in its proud 190-year history." Of course, there is no reason why the violation of
an established moral limit cannot have more than one
justifying cause, but the several causes advanced did not
all have the same bearing on the case for violation.
Therefore, the decision to package them together for
presentation damaged the *moral* presuasiveness (as distinguished from the *rhetorical* persuasiveness) and coherence of the argument.

First, the various "causes" cited were not equally
valid. Not many persons were inclined to condemn the
President for wanting to protect the withdrawing American
troops, even if they believed they should not have been
there in the first place. But a sizeable number of Ameri-

cans rejected Vietnamization and doubted both the justice and the possibility of winning the war on American terms. And there were some—unfortunately too few—who were nauseated by the inflated and perverse national egotism represented in the willingness to sacrifice so much life and treasure rather than risk the supposed danger of becoming a "second-rate power" and accepting what was alleged to be our first military defeat. That last reason in particular provides no justification at all for violating another nation's boundaries.

Second, as a result of this packaging, the morally questionable causes were allowed to ride in on the back of one that evidently was unassailable. Having established his initial argument on a proper concern for the safety of American servicemen, the President was able to employ the other "causes" in his argument without having to defend them.

Third, not all of the causes that might be presumed to be defensible in themselves necessarily justified this particular action. Let us assume that the threat to the withdrawing servicemen made the Cambodian action "necessary." Is it as clear that the incursion into Cambodia was really "necessary" to maintain U.S. prestige ("reputation for power") as a stabilizing factor in world politics? By no means. One is related to the other, but only in a minor way by comparison with the immediate threat to the departing GI's. The prestige of the United States, however important it might be, was not seriously threatened by the movement of Communist troops in Cambodia. Therefore, it could not serve as "just cause" for the penetration of the borders by U.S. forces. Nonetheless, Mr. Nixon implied that U.S. prestige was as intimately related to the necessity of action as was the security of the American troops.

Fourth, the determinations of "just intention" and "just proportion" are not the same for the several causes. How far into Cambodia do you intend to go? How long do you intend to stay? How much damage do you feel justified in causing or sustaining in order to achieve your purpose? The answers to these questions will be different for different "causes." Presumably (although not certainly) there would be less incursion and less damage if the cause was to defend the American troops than if it was to end the war on American terms. As we pointed out earlier, Mr. Nixon endeavored to cover himself on this point by defining the limits of U.S. intentions. But he made these intentions seem much less definite by presenting a variety of "just causes" that did not require the same limits. In so doing, he considerably weakened his moral argument.

How might the President have advanced a stronger and more coherent moral argument? Clearly, by resting his case only on the necessity of protecting the troops. The main requirements of his case then would have been to show (a) that the threat was as clear and formidable as he said it was, (b) that the Cambodian incursion was necessary to relieve the threat, (c) that it had a good chance of succeeding, and (d) that all other possibilities of relieving the threat had been tried.

Would this stronger and more coherent argument have been valid? We think not. The main weakness in it is that not all possibilities short of moving against the bases in Cambodia had been tried. Specifically, the U.S. had never made negotiating offers based on the premise that the one item of importance was the safe evacuation of its troops. Its offers always assumed that what we were willing to negotiate would not threaten our basic policy goals and would not permit the Communists to achieve theirs.

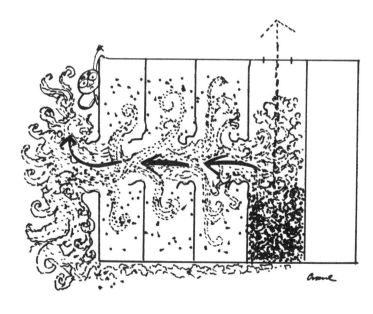

I had excellent reasons for doing what I did.

Therefore, Mr. Nixon could not claim that the incursion into Cambodia was made as a "last resort" for the sole purpose of safely evacuating U.S. troops. He had to offer other causes.

But were those other causes morally justified? Did Mr. Nixon show that Vietnamization, achieving U.S. policy goals, and maintaining U.S. prestige were valid causes for crossing Cambodia's borders? We have already indicated reasons for thinking that he did not.

In light of these considerations, we conclude that the speech as a moral argument not only lacked coherence but also failed in its avowed intent of presenting to the world just cause for the invasion of Cambodia.

Moral Reasoning After and Before

Statesmen should publicly give reasons for their violations of established rules and rights. They should do so because they owe an explanation to those whose rights have been violated, and because they owe an accounting to those whose power they have used. But a public defense is not prima facie evidence of moral seriousness. It may be nothing other than a public relations "snow job"—an occasion for making excuses for bad decisions or propaganda for those that are self-serving.

What is most important is that the public defense correspond to and report faithfully the process of moral deliberation that preceded and entered into the shaping of the decision. We are interested in the process of moral reasoning because we want to encourage moral seriousness and maturity of judgment in the course of making foreign policy decisions. The purpose is not to *feel* righteous about what we are doing, and certainly not to be self-righteous. Unless we are kidding ourselves, we know that "all our righteousnesses are as filthy rags," (Isa. 64:6, K.J.V.) and that our salvation is "not because of works, lest any man should boast." (Eph. 2:9) The purpose, rather, is to protect what has been committed to us in the trust of office, and at the same time to avoid or at least to minimize the harm that may be done to others in the fulfillment of that trust.

QUESTIONS FOR THOUGHT AND DISCUSSION

1. This chapter discusses the "just limits" for the legitimate use of force. Are there any "just limits" that should never be violated for any cause?

2. How seriously should states regard international law as a limit to their pursuit of justifiable national interests?

3. Do you feel that United States "spy ships" (like the "Pueblo") are justified in violating North Korean territorial waters for the purpose of gathering information? Why? Are Russian "trawlers" justified in violating U.S. territorial waters for the same reason?

4. Can you think of other moral problems for which the "just war" criteria would be helpful in the process of moral reasoning? What about euthanasia? abortion?

5 | The Role and Limits of Intervening Force

The Lessons of Painful Memories

Probably there is nothing we would like better than to put the memories of the Vietnam war behind us. It has been a disaster in more ways than we can count and in greater magnitude than we can measure. But there are important, indeed vital reasons why we must examine the memories and not simply repress them.[1]

One is that the war has given new insights into the depths of our national existence and consciousness, and has revealed a scarcely suspected sickness that must be treated and healed if we are to survive. Another is that Vietnam is but one instance of a type of war which is almost certain to break out—perhaps many times—in the future and beckon for United States involvement. We must prepare ourselves to reckon with that eventuality, lest we not only commit the same mistakes again, but also compound and multiply them. Our best preparation for the future is a thoughtful study of our past mistakes.

The second of these reasons will receive our main attention in this chapter, and the particular aspect on which we shall focus will be the role and limits of military force used by the United States as an intervening power. There is another major aspect: the criteria of wisdom and justification for the decision to intervene. However, we shall concentrate on the military question, because that is basic to both the decision to intervene and the conduct of the intervention.

Little Wars and Great Powers

But why should there be more wars of this type, and why should the U.S. be drawn into them? The answer to the first question is that there are many other "third world" countries with societal and governmental characteristics similar to those of South Vietnam. These societies are "underdeveloped" by twentieth-century standards, and important segments of their populations are eager to throw off the archaic, feudalistic (or tribal) structures that impede their "modernization"—their realization of the promise of technological competence and economic sufficiency. Also, these societies often have corrupt, repressive regimes that govern by brute force and torture and deny justice and freedom to the many in order to serve the interests of the privileged few. Societies with these characteristics breed revolutionaries who struggle to bring about their radical transformation.

The answer to the second question is that these societies are weak spots in the international political system. The prospect of their internal collapse tends to create a political vacuum which sucks in the power conflict among the giants of world politics. The Soviet Union, the United States, and the People's Republic of China all are drawn to the points of weakness, sometimes in hopes of exploiting the deteriorating situation to their own advantage, but often in the defensive effort to prevent an adverse change in the world balance of power.

It is pointless to urge the United States simply to resolve on principle to stay out of such conflicts. Doubtless the U.S. cannot and should not try to play the role of "global policeman," but the plain fact—not easily alterable in the foreseeable future—is that the U.S. is a global power. Instead of pretending that we can avoid future involvement in affairs outside our own borders, we should develop a more responsible understanding of how power works and how it does not work, of where to apply it and where not to apply it. Above all, we should learn to exercise greater discipline in using military force.

"No Substitute for Victory"

What are the moral and practical considerations pertinent to the uses of intervening military force? An answer of striking clarity was offered in the testimony of General Mark Clark before a subcommittee of the Senate Judiciary Committee investigating the conduct of the Korean War:

> "Once our leaders, our authorized leaders, the President and Congress, decide that fight we must, in my opinion we should fight without any holds barred whatsoever.
>
> "We should fight to win, and we should not go in for a limited war where we put our limited man-power against the unlimited hordes of Communist manpower which they are willing to expend lavishly, and do. . . .
>
> "If fight we must, let's go in there and shoot the works for victory with everything at our disposal." [2]

The proposal is that once we are committed to a war, we should set aside all other considerations—especially those that are labeled "political" and even including those that pertain to important domestic needs—and press toward complete victory at the earliest moment by throwing into the fight every resource of men and material we can muster. General Douglas MacArthur summed up the point (and his recommended policy for the Korean War) in the now-famous slogan: "In war there is no substitute for victory." That is the rule for every war, and therefore it is the rule for intervening power in a Vietnam-type war. Win it. Win it big. And when you have won it, get out and come home.

The proposal seems reasonable enough. After all, in war a nation does not seek its own defeat, nor does it normally aim for a stalemate. To the contrary, when a nation decides to employ such extreme means as war in the conduct of foreign affairs, it surely must intend to break the power of the opponent to attack or even to resist.

Yet the administrations that conducted the Vietnamese intervention apparently were not completely sold on the applicability of the "shoot the works" principle, even though they seemed to subscribe to that basic ideology. Notwithstanding allegations of the "dove" critics to the contrary, the United States fought a limited war in Vietnam. It did not throw in all the troops it could have mustered. It did not invade North Vietnam or "seal off" the harbor at Haiphong. It did not "bomb North Vietnam back to the Stone Age" or "pave it from one end to the other," as some military men and politicians advocated. It did not attack Communist sanctuaries in Cambodia until after they had been there at least five years. It did not use nuclear weapons.

The reason for this restraint was neither failure of nerve nor lack of means or opportunity. It was not a deliberate "no win" policy. Rather, it had something to do with the fact that these administrations gradually became aware of limits to the role and uses of intervening military force. They saw the limits coming into focus in

Vietnam itself, in the international setting of the Vietnam conflict, in the total range of U.S. foreign policy commitments, and in the domestic conflicts of American society. They never disconnected themselves sufficiently from the "victory" point of view to ask how all of those limiting features fit together, and therefore they continued to make some foolish, indeed tragic decisions. But they did come to realize that a single-minded, blinders-on, overwhelming application of military power was neither a practicable nor a morally responsible way to bring that mournful conflict to an end.

Limits to Military Power

We must look at those limiting features more closely. In doing so we must bear in mind the dual nature of these "wars of national liberation": they are revolutionary conflicts in which members of the society fight each other and some of them fight against the official government; they are international events that seem to outside parties to have some bearing on the international balance of power.

A Supporting Role Only

Military intervention by the United States in "wars of national liberation" settings can be useful for only two purposes: (1) as counter-intervention to restrain another foreign power bent on exploiting the situation for its own advantage; (2) as a "holding operation" to permit the threatened government to attend to problems of social renewal and reconstruction.

The general conditions necessary to achieve these two purposes are too complicated and extensive to be discussed here, but we must cite one specific condition absolutely essential to useful military intervention: the host government must possess both the determination and the competence to deal directly with the social sources of disruption. It must not content itself with efforts to control the symptoms. If the host government is corrupt and cannot or will not purge itself; if it wants the intervener to carry the burden while refusing to impose sacrifices on itself and its supporters; if it pretends to work at creating a new climate of freedom while imprisoning the non-Communist political opposition and censoring all criticism in the press; if it installs informers in classrooms and churches and clubs and encourages its policemen to use brutal methods of torture; if it protects great landholders and factory-owners against the impoverished peasants and workers whom they have exploited and degraded, there is no practical contribution that intervening military power can make to the achievement of the basic political objectives of wholeness and justice and stability. Moreover, it is hard to imagine a moral justification for attempting to defeat the opponents of such a regime.

"Winning" in a Vietnam-type situation is not equivalent to defeat of the enemy. There can be no real "victory" until the conditions that create enemies within the society—the conditions that make brothers enemies to brothers—are changed. That is a work of profound social transformation, not of mere conquest, and it must be performed by the people of the society themselves working to shape an authoritative social and political structure. The military power of the intervener may help in the ways indicated above, but it cannot produce the goals.

On Not Shooting the Works

The "shoot the works" argument advanced by General Clark probably makes a great deal of sense in a war between massed field armies, especially if military or industrial installations afford large and relatively distinct targets. But it makes little military sense in counter-insurgency warfare, and it may become the occasion for mass murder and wanton destruction.

1) Guerrilla combat groups are too small and too mobile to be effective targets for heavy weapons. They hit and run, nibble at weak spots, steal weapons and supplies, and then fade into the jungle or into the people before the big guns or B-52 bombers can pin them down.

2) Guerrillas fight in the midst of the population, sometimes terrorizing them to prove that the government cannot defend them, sometimes using them as camouflage or shields, sometimes recruiting them to their ranks by fair means or foul.

3) When Vietnamese fight Vietnamese, how can the Americans tell who is friend and who is enemy, or who is combatant and who noncombatant? The peasant farmer quietly working the rice paddies by day may emerge from his hut by night clad in the black pajamas of the Viet Cong. The ten-year-old boy who shines the GI's shoes may be mapping the location of troops and weapons. The intelligence officer in the government battalion may be feeding top secret information to the North Vietnamese.

What does all of this mean for the "shoot the works" approach of an intervener with massive firepower? It means first that the firepower cannot be directed at the insurgents without targeting the host population, and that is exactly what has happened: "free fire zones," "suspected Viet Cong strongholds" (i.e. Vietnamese villages), "We had to destroy the city in order to save it." It means also that the distinctions between friend and foe among people who look alike to the foreign "allies" lose their preciseness if not their reality. The response of one of the witnesses to the My Lai massacre paints a picture we never should forget: What difference is there between the Vietnamese and the enemy? No difference. They are all "enemy." Kill them all.

With no serious prospect for distinguishing and isolating legitimate targets, massive firepower is irrational mass destruction. It is not an effective means of winning the war.[3]

International Implications

The United States must tailor its uses of intervening power to the political objective and the military conditions of the society where the war is taking place, but it must also qualify those military decisions with reference to their implications for the broader picture of international politics.

Little brown brothers, we have liberated you!   We bring you peace, friendship, freedom, and . . .   Sir!

1) Military measures that seem important to the war should not be undertaken if they would create the risk of serious reprisals from states whose interests would thereby be directly threatened. Bombing and mining the harbor at Haiphong might well have resulted in the sinking of Russian ships. An invasion of North Vietnam almost certainly would have invoked a flood of a million or so "volunteers" from Communist China. Similar situations can occur in other settings.

2) If the U.S. really were going to "shoot the works," it would use its nuclear weapons. If it is going to use its military power responsibly, it will not use nuclear warfare. The issue here is not primarily whether there are suitable targets in counter-insurgency warfare, although that certainly is an issue. Rather, it is whether a major world power should use such comparatively remote situa-

Yes, Lieutenant.   There are none   Can't win 'em all.
                          of 'em left, sir.

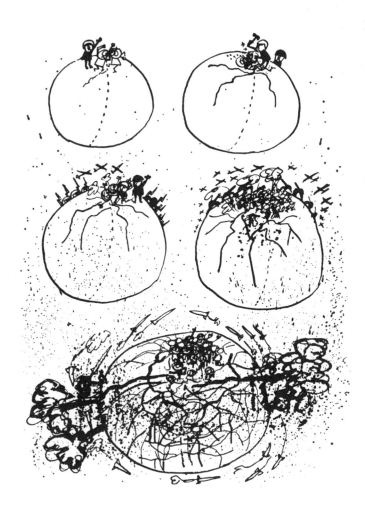

tions to cross the "nuclear threshold." The question is one of breaking a psychological barrier of incomparable importance for limiting the destructiveness of war.

Let us remember that the dreaded nuclear weapons have been used in warfare only twice, and no nation has used them since August 1945. If some state creates a new precedent for their use, it will then be much easier for that state and for others to yield to the temptation to use them again and again. When one considers those horrible prospects, one surely must agree that it is better to absorb some tragic but limited losses in order to forestall weapon usages which would result in much greater, perhaps unlimited destruction of life in the future.

3) The U.S. may have too many irons in the fire of global politics, but even if it pulls some out, it still cannot focus on a Vietnam-type war as though "winning it" were the one item of overriding importance in its foreign policy. The U.S. simply cannot put all other considerations aside and invest everything in the winning of that type of war. If it does so, it becomes vulnerable all over the rest of the globe—Berlin, the Middle East, Latin America—and concedes the advantage to the Soviet Union.

The Environmental Approach

There is a much more effective and responsible approach to the uses and limits of intervening power than the one conveyed by the slogan: "In war there is no substitute for victory." It is the one set forth in the first chapter, where we described foreign policy in terms of the metaphor of interaction with the environment. This approach enables us to look at the wholeness and con-

creteness of the world in which foreign policy is conducted. It reminds us that the political objective always
is primary, and that "winning" is important only if it
serves that objective. It teaches us to look at the actual
conditions under which military power is to be used, and
to determine whether the avalanche of death carried by
massive firepower is a rational means or a totally irrational one. It forces us to look at the connecting links
between the particular war and the other elements of the
international political system. It insists that the United
States hold in view the whole collection of its responsibilities—those that arise out of the global spread of its
power and those that arise out of the needs of its own
people.

For all of these reasons the "environmental" approach to the uses of intervening power is far more
realistic—and more responsible in moral attitudes—than
the "victory" approach. There is also another reason.
When one looks at intervention in these terms, he does not
allow himself to be caught up in wishful thinking about
"winning and getting out." If winning means the slow,
painful process of rebuilding a society, and not simply
the defeat of the opponent, then the United States as
intervener is going to be in for the long haul. If the
U.S. is unwilling to make that long-range commitment, it
should stay out (which is good advice in most cases
anyway).

The Discipline of Restraint

Of course when we speak in such terms, we are
talking about restraint in the use of power. The "shoot
the works" approach is easy. It requires no disciplined
withholding of power ready at hand. The "environmental"

approach is hard. And it is especially hard for a people (like ourselves) inclined to impatience in the conduct of foreign affairs. But there is no way to cut the tension of international conflict once and for all. That is the great temptation and delusion of the "victory" approach: to believe that you can overpower the enemy, dictate your terms, and return home to sit under your vine and fig tree with none to make you afraid (Micah 4:4). The truth is that man can produce no such victory. Partial and temporary victories, perhaps, but none that once and for all overcomes the evil that threatens us and makes us insecure.

If we were to study the New Testament more carefully, we would know that. The final victory that removes the tensions of human existence is a work of God, not man, and it is beyond history as we know it. In the interim the true victory, the only real victory that we know, is the victory of faith over sin and doubt and despair. If, through faith, we lay hold of that victory and the peace that follows it, we shall be able to maintain our poise and our discipline as we perform our tasks of using and limiting power in a world that continues to be a world of tribulation. We shall not be surprised to meet tribulation, for we have been forewarned: "In the world you have tribulation." (John 16:33) But neither shall we act in rash, destructive haste because of it, for we know that he who forewarned us has overcome the world.

QUESTIONS FOR THOUGHT AND DISCUSSION

1. What are the three most important lessons you have learned from the Vietnam war?

2. Do you feel that the American public are willing to apply to our own wartime actions the same standards

we apply to those who fight against us? Give evidence for your answer.

3. Suppose we intervene again in someone else's war at great cost in lives of our fighting men, and then discover that the grounds for intervention were not as justifiable as we thought they were. Should we cut our losses and withdraw, or fight on to victory so that our men will not "have died in vain"?

4. What does "victory" mean in a Vietnam-type war?

5. Can a war be fought justifiably if it is next to impossible to distinguish friend from foe and combatant from noncombatant?

6. Does the New Testament assure us that there will be peace among the nations?

6 | Communism and Reconciliation

Reconciliation and International Relations

God has called all Christians to the ministry of reconciliation in a broken world. That is Biblical truth that cannot be denied or evaded by those who confess Christian faith and believe themselves summoned to a life of Christian discipleship. In the first chapter we referred to Paul's declaration of this calling in 2 Corinthians 5, and we insisted that it must be carried through in the Christian's political involvement as well as in all other areas of his life. Specifically, Christians should seek out and become actively involved in bringing to reality the linkage between their mission of reconciliation and the nation's foreign policy.

We recall Jesus' observation that "Those who are well have no need of a physician, but those who are sick." (Mark 2:17) Where is there sickness in this world? Is it only in souls and bodies, or is it not also in every form of human relationship, including especially the relationships among nations? If the degree of illness determines the need for healing, then surely the conduct of international relations is the neediest of all! And are not the leaves of the tree of life "for the healing of the nations"? (Rev. 22:2) Can we, in good Christian conscience, turn aside from the call to find some way to shape foreign policy judgments with moral insights—insights that derive from God's healing work in man's sinful society?

Some Serious Complaints

Challenges to apply moral insight to foreign policy decisions become more difficult—and usually more objectionable—when they become concrete and specific. In our own experience, the ultimate test of this Biblically-defined calling is to draw the relationships between the United States and political Communism into the context of reconciliation. Given the history of those relationships, and given the deeply hostile and suspicious attitudes on both sides, the proposal seems doomed to frustration and defeat.

One complaint against the proposal is that it is hopelessly naïve. It does not face up to the fact that Communism is a hardened doctrinal system, that the actions of Communists are directed by that hard doctrine, that Communists individually and as groups are political evangelists for their doctrine, and that they will not compromise their ultimate objective of seeing their doctrinal system prevail throughout the world. To them reconciliation is the classless society—a goal which can be achieved only after all their opponents have either been destroyed or purged of the corruption of the old order. Agreements, treaties, adjustments, and bargains are but tactical maneuvers arranged to serve the ultimate end.

A second complaint is that reconciliation means cooperation and compromise with the forces of evil. How can we think of reconciliation with a movement that subordinates every consideration of truth, freedom, mercy, life, and honor to the one goal of the victory of the revolution? How can we be reconciled with governments that are responsible for the war against Finland, the deal with Hitler (against Poland), the Katyn Massacres, the subjugation of Eastern Europe, the suppression of Hungary in 1956 and of Czechoslovakia in 1968, the decimation of entire social classes in Russia, China, and Cuba, the invasion of South Korea, the efforts to subvert governments all over the world?

A third complaint against the proposal is that reconciliation is a "no win" policy. If the Communists are determined to win, why should we not be equally determined? Is not an effort at reconciliation a concession that their way is right, at least for them, or that the differences and issues are not worth struggling over?

A Look at Communists and "World Communism"

Basic to the first complaint is the insistence that Communists are ruled by their doctrine in everything they do. We must challenge the absoluteness of that assumption while admitting that Communists are, of course, strongly influenced by their doctrine.

If they were completely and entirely controlled by their doctrine, they would always think and act the same way and for the same reasons. They would always cooperate with each other and never disagree or fight among themselves. But the plain facts are that Communists across the world differ from each other in many respects. Sometimes they even disagree over Marxist *doctrine,* and accuse each other of being "revisionists"! In one celebrated case —the border dispute between Russia and China—the two leading Communist states actually used military force against each other.

Non-doctrinal factors usually are at the roots of these differences, and of the various non-doctrinal factors, none has been more important than nationalism. While Joseph Stalin was dictator of Russia, Communism was for the most part a unified world movement under his control. One spoke of it as the "Communist monolith," with its controlling center in Moscow. Even then it was not perfectly monolithic, as Yugoslavia demonstrated when it asserted its independence as a Communist state in 1948.

Since the time of Stalin's preeminence, Communists have come into power in a number of states, and their success in doing so has broken the near-absolute control of the Soviet Union over the world Communist movement. Now Russia and China compete for the favor of smaller Communist states, and the smaller states often play the two giants off against each other to see how much they can get out of both of them. Fidel Castro played that game quite successfully for awhile.

What this development means is that when Communists are faced with the necessity of governing states, they find that they must pay direct attention to *national interests,* sometimes at the expense of commitment to the cause of *world revolution.* The pursuit of their own interests at times puts them on a collision course with the interests of other Communists states. In other words, they are behaving like *states,* not simply like *Communists.*

An astute foreign policy planner in a non-Communist state will pay careful attention to this difference. He will not minimize the influence of ideology, because it is in fact there. But he will encourage Communist states to behave primarily as states, that is, to define their goals more in political terms than in ideological terms. On the one hand, that will modify and retard pressures toward "world Communist unity." On the other, it will afford more credibility to agreements between Communist and non-Communist states over matters of common interest.

There are other important factors that modify and sometimes contradict the ideological determination of behavior. It is clear, for example, that as Communist societies exist through time they inevitably undergo historical changes, as do all societies. Generations of leaders succeed each other, as do generations of subjects. The aims and experiences of the different generations are not the same, nor are they related in the same way to the historic revolutionary event. Material success dilutes the sympathy which members of the prospering society feel for the oppressed "proletariat" in other parts of the world. Lack of material success creates impatience with foreign adventurism and a demand for consumer goods in preference to guns and missiles. Weariness with official excuses, with repression, with propaganda, produces cynicism toward doctrinal orthodoxy and encourages a more pragmatic interest in evidence of achievement.

We cannot say for certain what these changes and differences mean, or whether they are good or bad. Sometimes we are too optimistic about the implications of change in Communist societies. But it may be that those who are aware of the historical character of Communist movements and societies are in the final analysis more realistic than the hard-nosed types who insist that these movements and societies always must be understood and responded to on the basis of their ideological doctrines. If our opponents (and we ourselves) are indeed driven by an exclusivistic, imperialistic ideology, there is not much sense in talking about reconciliation. But if they show evidence of complexity, changeability, adaptability (and if we do, also), then the proposal to draw the relationships into a context of reconciliation may be the most sensible that can be made.

A Hard Look at Ourselves

The second complaint is that reconciliation means cooperation and compromise with the forces of evil. One way to answer this objection would be to point to the positive accomplishments in Marxist societies, such as universal education, equal opportunity for women, full employment, abolition of prostitution, and spectacular scientific advances. These achievements, unfortunately, do not erase the realities of ruthlessness, repression, and governmental management of thought and life. Therefore, they do not overcome the objections to cooperation with such societies.

Biblically understood, however, the possibilities for the reconciliation of human beings to each other depend on their common need of the righteousness of God. Why do they need the righteousness of God? Because they have none of their own to use as a claim against each other. Paul asked the Christians in Rome, "What then? Are we Jews any better off? No, not at all; for I have already charged that all men, both Jews and Greeks, are under the power of sin, as it is written: 'None is righteous, no, not one.' " (Rom. 3:9–10) We would be entirely true to his meaning if we paraphrased his words, "All men, Americans and Russians and Chinese, are under the power of sin."

That does not mean there are no moral distinctions at all between non-Communists and Communists, but it does mean that we cannot reduce the distinctions to a simple contrast between the good and the evil. Perhaps we should direct to ourselves the reprimand of Jesus to the righteous would-be killers of the woman taken in adultery: "Let him who is without sin among you be the first to throw a stone at her." (John 8:7)

If we take a hard and honest look at ourselves, as many of our young people are demanding that we do, we shall have to confess that our behavior does not conform so neatly to the complimentary image we have of ourselves. Our society was built not only on the "initiative and courage of the hardy pioneers," but also on centuries of massive injustice to Indians and Blacks and immigrants and white sharecroppers. Our foreign policy supports some elements of freedom in the world, but it also supports a substantial number of dictatorial regimes. We have indeed protected weaker countries from attack, but we also have intervened in weaker countries to serve our own purposes.

This kind of honest self-examination will not excuse the sins of our opponents, but it certainly should curtail objections to seeking reconciliation that are based on unjustified moral self-congratulation.

"Win" and "No Win" Policies

The third complaint is that to seek reconciliation is a "no win" policy in the global struggle against Communism. We have already disposed of one of the necessary assumptions of this view, namely, that "world Communism" is a unified, seamless movement with one spirit and one nerve center. We need also to expose the fallacy of another of its necessary assumptions—that Communism is the cause of all the conflict in the world, so that when we have defeated Communism we shall have taken care of the basic problem. This assumption is set forth with unapologetic bluntness by Senator Barry Goldwater in his widely read book, *Why Not Victory?* He writes, "The only real disarmament will come when the cause for arms is removed. In our case that cause is communism. In the Soviets' case, that cause is the free world." [1]

At last, national security, just for the two of us, Eve—
Speak to me, Eve!

That assertion is more in the realm of myth than of fact. It is quite true, of course, that Communists are aggressive and disruptive, but the movement would not even exist were there not conditions of human degradation and deprivation to call it into existence and make it seem appealing as a solution. According to Senator Goldwater, there are revolutions because there are Communists; if we "defeat" Communism we eliminate the cause of revolutions. The real fact of the matter, however, is that there are Communists because there are revolution-inspiring conditions. Millions of people throughout the world are living under conditions of colonial oppression, racial oppression, economic oppression, and political oppression. These forms of oppression are very real to the people who experience them; they were not invented by Communist propaganda. These oppressed people want out. The worldwide communications media and the successes of technology have shown them that life does not have to be like this. They will not "calm down" until the real causes of their distress have been dealt with in a manner and to an extent that meets their needs.

Communists make every effort to exploit these conditions. Sometimes they provide the spark that ignites the dry tinder. Sometimes they try to capture and subvert non-Communist revolutions. But they have demonstrated no mysterious power to produce violent illness in a basically healthy social body.

A "win" policy that is to be taken seriously is one that deals with the true sources of social unrest. It is a positive policy, committed to justice in human relationships and to the political and economic development of "underdeveloped" countries to the point where they can function as basically self-dependent, self-governing elements in international society. A "no win" policy is one that avoids the fundamental diagnosis and tries to deal only with the symptoms. It is a purely negative policy which assumes that if only we can develop enough resolution to defeat those who are to blame for the mess in the world, then everyone can live in peace and harmony and plenty.

To seek reconciliation in foreign policy is a "win" policy, because it is committed to the building up of genuine community in world affairs. Those who espouse this method know that there can be no order and peace in the world without justice, and they pursue justice both for its own sake and as a means to order and peace. They are not thereby "soft" on aggressors who attempt to force other people to submit to their wills, but they know that the defeat or control of such aggressors is not the

How can honorable men cope with a ruthless enemy?

He is fanatical, diabolic, inhuman.

Stern measures are necessary. Fight fire with fire!

final answer to the world's problems. They know also that such aggressors are not found in only one ideological camp.

The Meaning of the Method

When some persons begin to see through the myths that allow us always to approve of our own behavior and disapprove of that of our opponents, they tend to plunge to the other extreme. If they discover that not everything about American conduct is holy and just, they may develop a love for morbid diatribes against what they take to be the characteristic and inherent moral perverseness of their country. If they suddenly see that heavy American investments in foreign countries often lead to virtual American control over the economies of those countries, to support of corrupt and repressive regimes, and to use

We must learn to think as he thinks.

Plot and scheme as he does.

of American boys in uniform to protect those investments, they may flip over the coin of anti-Communism and indict our economic system as the source of all the evil in the world.

These are overreactions. They may be as dishonest and ultimately as dangerous as the evils they reject. They have nothing in common with what we propose as a method of reconciliation in foreign policy. To attempt to clarify this method, let us say what we do not mean and what we do mean when we speak of drawing relationships with the Soviet Union and other Communist elements into a context of reconciliation.

We do not mean that Christians should suppose they can reconcile the deep doctrinal differences between Christian faith and Marxism, particularly those differences having to do with belief in God, the nature of man,

Act as he acts.
Hate as he hates.

the explanation of evil in human society, and the hope for the future. We do not mean that non-Communist countries should simply abandon their interests in cases of conflict or that they should disarm unilaterally. We do not mean that the United States and other non-Communist states should supinely give way before every harsh threat, or that they should avert their gaze from Communist repression and atrocities.

We do mean, however, that the conduct of foreign policy should seek to normalize relationships with these states and not insist on perpetuating a condition of bristling hostility and, in some cases, of isolation or "quarantine." We mean that the United States should identify and nurture areas of significant common interest, and not concentrate on and dramatize only the conflicts of interest. We mean that the U.S. should patiently support and build up communications and agreements about procedures (and in some cases the trade relationships) with Communist states, and not assume that such relationships are inherently immoral or that they work only to the benefit of the Communists.

To seek reconciliation assumes that conflicts of interest are real and not imaginary, and that all dealings will reflect the relative power of the interacting states. It does not assume that all disputes could easily be harmonized if only we all would "be sensible," "trust one another," and "sit down together and talk things other." But it insists that the relationships do not reduce to *nothing except* conflict.

There are, in fact, common interests, unifying forces, beginnings for bridge-building over the chasms that separate us. The realities of power and interest exist, but they are not the only realities. There are real factors of community among the contestants. Undaunted by the weakness and relative ineffectiveness of such factors, those who urge reconciliation side with these factors as the forces of the future, and shepherd and develop their strength so that they may play a truly healing role in the midst of international antagonism. When foreign policy is conducted on the basis of these assumptions and with this intent, it shares in the reconciling work of God.

Moral Principles of Political Action

Because statesmen know that they are responsible for the nation's interests, they make central to their concept of political responsibility the following moral principle: in situations of international conflict, act always in such a manner as to support the national interests. But they do not necessarily make all decisions on the basis of that consideration alone. They may modify the principle to take account of the interests of others and/or of the total system of international relationships that sustains both them and their opponents. In such cases they should state their operating principles as follows: when pursuing the national interest in situations of international conflict, use the national power in such ways as to support and not impair the future possibilities of community and cooperation among the present antagonists.

That principle is always appropriate to the conduct of foreign policy between the United States and Communist countries. It is never unrealistic. It is never morally wrong. It is never more dangerous than its alternatives.

QUESTIONS FOR THOUGHT AND DISCUSSION

1. In the midst of practically every conflict, one can discern some forces that promote reconciliation and

wholeness. Are these forces evidence of the working of God in our own history? Give a Biblical basis for your answer. What evidence of such forces can you see in the relations of the U.S. with the Soviet Union? with the People's Republic of China? with Cuba?

2. Improved relationships with some Communist governments arouse jealousies and suspicions in other Communist governments. How does Russia view U.S. efforts to improve relations with China? How does China view improvements in U.S.-Russian relations? How do you weigh the danger of this suspicion, on the one hand, against the value of improved relationships on the other?

3. What is wrong and what is right about improving trade relations with Communist countries?

7 | Truth in the Public Squares

Honesty and Policy

Are governments ever justified in falsifying the truth in the course of conducting their foreign policy? Strange question. Not only strange, but naïve as well. Do we suppose that there are any governments anywhere that do not deal in falsehoods, not only *some* of the time, but *most* of the time? Recall Pontius Pilate's response to Jesus when Jesus said to him, "For this I was born, and for this I have come into the world, to bear witness to the truth. Every one who is of the truth hears my voice." Pilate countered by asking simply, "What is truth?" (John 18:37b–38) To Pilate that was probably no profound philosophical question, but simply a shrugging of the shoulders by a practical man of politics who made decisions not in terms of moral right and wrong but in terms of calculation of power and advantage. In that respect isn't Pontius Pilate the prototype of the political decision-maker in every age and culture? Aren't diplomats and presidents and prime ministers disposed to lie and deceive and distort as a matter of course (and perhaps as a responsibility of office) when to do so will promote the interests of the countries they represent?

The situation probably isn't as bad as we think it is, but it might be hard to prove that it isn't! Even if it is that bad, we cannot dismiss our question. Integrity in governmental communication is of great importance to the quality of life in the national society as well as to the quality of relationships among states, and the issue therefore is one that the Christian conscience is bound to probe.

Just after the Cuban missile crisis—a time when our government engaged in deception for what it thought were very good reasons—Arthur Sylvester, the Assistant Secretary of Defense for Public Affairs, said, ". . . it is in the government's right, if necessary, to lie to save itself when it is going up to nuclear war." [1] Is a government (we repeat) ever justified in falsifying the truth in the course of conducting its foreign policy? If so, what determines whether its reasons are "very good" ones?

Truth and Community

Why make so much fuss over falsehood in the conduct of foreign policy, especially when we expect it as a matter of course? To help us with our perspective on the question, let us consider the profound insights of Isaiah 59, especially verses 14–15:

> Justice is turned back,
>   and righteousness stands afar off;
> for truth has fallen in the public squares,
>   and uprightness cannot enter.
> Truth is lacking, and he who departs from evil makes
>   himself a prey.

"Truth has fallen in the public squares." The primary reference was to the courts of law, in which no one—as the writer saw it—could get a fair trial. Why couldn't he? Because just legal procedure depends on truth and honesty. Those qualities had been withdrawn from the center of the society, and their withdrawal had resulted in the collapse of the institutions of which they were the foundation. No one was secure in his rights; no one could be compelled to perform his duties. Then and now, where there is no truth, there is no accepted order, and every man becomes his own judge, his own legislator (a law to himself), his own executive, his own first and last line of defense. This condition compels a man to violate the moral law in order to survive, for where "truth is lacking . . . he who departs from evil makes himself a prey."

Truth is not just "telling it like it is." Truth is a relationship of trust and openness in which we confidently expect forthrightness from others and do not penalize them for it, and in which we freely express forthrightness without fear of reprisal. Truth is community, and truth is covenantal. It is what we need to exist as free and whole human beings. It is what we owe to one another in the bond of trust and love. Lying, deceiving, and distorting are violations of the covenant. Practiced frequently or consistently, they destroy the community and with it the possibility of a free, morally responsive, integral human existence. The first reason why lying (in its several forms) is wrong is that it is a betrayal of trust and loyalty. The second reason is that it undermines the possibilities of human existence as life in community.

Truth and Diplomacy

At first glance, those considerations may not seem to have much relevance to foreign policy. States have no primary covenantal obligations to each other. In international relations one in fact cannot "depart from evil" without "making himself a prey." But the first glance is somewhat misleading. With more careful observation we recognize several considerations that make the free use of falsehood in international politics questionable for states.

History begins with us.

In Ur we can build a Great city—

the first civilization.

God and man will be watching us.

Then let's show 'em how
we can Bash our enemies!

First, if those who have the responsibility for the conduct of foreign policy make a regular habit of lying in diplomatic representations, they will—at least in the long run—serve the interests of their country very badly. Their statements of intention will be disbelieved, their promises and commitments discounted, their solemn agreements distrusted.[2]

Second, states do in fact enter into political and legal covenants. They sign treaties, form alliances, and join international organizations. All of these covenant relationships carry with them reciprocal expectations concerning truth-telling, at least so far as communications pertain to the interests and commitments of the covenant.

Third, some states have long histories of friendly, trustful, and supportive relations with each other, whether they have entered into formal covenant agreements or not. Truth is an expectation of these relationships. Lying, deception, and distortion are perceived as betrayals of friendship and confidence.

Fourth, if the people and the governors of a national society aspire to live in a world where conflicts can be resolved more readily by procedural means and with much less reliance on the threat or use of armed force, they must create the conditions of trust that support authoritative international institutions. They must commit themselves to the establishment of truth in the "public squares" of world intercourse. They must build that commitment into their foreign policy procedures, and not return to falsehood for some of the trivial pretexts that so often are dignified by the appeal to "national interest."

Despite these important considerations, international society is not a community fully committed to truth. One state cannot be thoroughly honest all the time unless

all other states are as well. Moreover, it is undeniable that foreign policy decision-makers see their primary covenant obligations as being to their own states and people in cases of conflict with obligations to other states and peoples. Therefore, we should not be surprised or necessarily morally outraged if on a sufficiently grave occasion even the most honorable statesman declines to "tell the truth, the whole truth, and nothing but the truth."

The People Enter the Picture

But not all parts of the picture are here. A major one is missing. Thus far we have been speaking as though the central moral issue were the deception of the *foreign adversary.* However, most of the occasions for raising the problem of lying in recent years have involved the charge of the government's lying to *its own people.* One major apparent exception occurred in 1960 with the shooting down of an American U-2 spy plane over Soviet Russia. The Eisenhower administration first claimed that the plane was making meteorological observations and had flown off course. Then Soviet Premier Khrushchev produced proof of the plane's true mission and exposed the government's cover stories as falsehoods.

"At this point," writes John Spanier, "the Administration reversed itself. In a move unprecedented in diplomatic history, it admitted that Khrushchev had been correct, that the U-2 pilot had been taking aerial photographs of the Soviet Union, and that it had lied in its previous announcement." [3] Even in that case, however, we were less troubled by the moral question of lying to the Russians than by the embarrassment over being caught publicly at both spying and lying.

Traditionally, the moral problem was in fact seen as one of speaking deceitfully to the enemy. The people were not in the picture because foreign policy was none of their business. With the advent of representative democracy, however, foreign policy became the people's business, and the people thereby became part of the foreign policy process. They claimed the "right to know" the truth about what the government was doing in the conduct of foreign affairs. Moreover, the theorists of democracy often assumed that a well-informed public would keep the makers of foreign policy honest and on the right track.

Representative democracy puts new pressures on governments and subjects them to strong temptations. For one thing, governments regularly have to decide whether to give the public no information or false information in order to avoid tipping their hand to the opponent. It is not possible to give the home TV audience the truth while withholding it from the Russians. Secondly, governments dependent on public support are tempted to manipulate public attitudes and moods with propaganda and public relations techniques and emotional harangues when support has to be evoked or recovered.

According to John M. Blum, President Woodrow Wilson succumbed to this temptation in the attempt to whip up reluctant public sentiment for U.S. participation in World War I. As his instrument, he created the Committee on Public Information, which controlled censorship and information, but also

> . . . executed a campaign of propaganda without precedent in American history. They purveyed two major thoughts: one . . . that Americans fought only for freedom and democracy; the other . . . that the Germans, 'Huns' all, were creatures of the devil

attempting by the deliberate, lustful perpetration of atrocities to conquer the world. . . . At once reflecting and intensifying the unreasoning attitudes of men at war, the C.P.I. suggested daily that German spies had ears to every wall, German agents keys to every factory.[4]

Although both problems present serious moral difficulties, yielding to the second temptation is obviously less open to justification than yielding to the first.

When Truth Falls

There are two reasons why a government's false dealings with its own people are morally more questionable than false dealing with the opponent. The first is that the covenant obligation between the government and the people is clear and undeniable, whereas in relation to the opponent its existence can only be confessed in faith. The second is that a government's lying to its own people undermines the trust which supports the community and its institutions, whereas lying to the opponent is essentially a survival technique in a hostile and ungoverned world.

We know something firsthand about the second reason, because we have seen in recent years the collapse of public confidence, the epidemic of suspicion, the alienation of youth, the pervasive social malaise which went hand-in-hand with the widening of the "credibility gap" in the late sixties and early seventies. We identify the "credibility gap" primarily with the administration of President Lyndon Johnson, because it was that administration's conduct of the Vietnam war that led many Americans to perceive an increasing disparity between what they were being told about the war and what actually seemed to be happening. But the gap was present before Johnson, and it has not been healed by his successor.

However, it is not our purpose here to indict any administration. We shall leave to others to decide whether the "Pentagon Papers"—revealed by The New York *Times* on June 13, 1971—actually document as much wholesale deception of the American people as the critics claim they do. Our purpose, rather, is to point out that a government does not really serve the national interest if the foreign policy methods that it feels impelled to adopt for reasons of national security work to destroy the very national community it is trying to preserve. When truth falls in the public squares, the society is likely to fall with it.

Approaches to the Problem

How can we resolve this very complex problem? Perhaps we could resolve it simply by declaring that governments ought never to lie, deceive, or distort, regardless of the consequences. That way the government would never communicate falsely to foe, friend, or family, and it would never violate the covenant obligations of truth. If the national society were to undergo serious disruption and disintegration, it would not be because truth had fallen in the public squares.

That would be a consistent approach to moral judgment, but its consistency also would downgrade, if not cancel out, another aspect of moral obligation, namely, the responsibility of policy-makers to protect the security interests of the society. We can assume, moreover, that if moral considerations enter into the head of the policy-maker at all (and they do), they will be shaped primarily by his sense of responsibility to office and country, and only secondarily by commitment to moral principles and rules. That being so, we may get somewhere if we discuss moral judgments in terms of concrete responsibilities, but we probably will get nowhere if we try to impose invariable rules.

How, then, are the moral responsibilities of the policy-maker to be fulfilled in situations where truth is likely to be a casualty of action supporting national interests? The operative rule for policy-makers is to do what is necessary to support the national interest. However, as we have seen, "national interest" in the traditional sense is too simplistic a justification for falsehood in governmental communications. Lying to the opponent is lying to the people at home, and a regular practice of lying to the people at home can destroy the foundations of government and community. That is hardly the "national interest"!

Some Guidelines

Perhaps at this point we should humbly confess that there is no clear and confident way out of the moral dilemma. We are living in a broken and fallen world where selfishness infects the motives of the best of us, and where the noblest of men and women are led by tragic situations to do out of moral necessity things they consider morally repugnant. Granted that human condition, we can assume that governments will make what they believe to be justifiable decisions to lie to their adversaries and even to their constituencies.

If so, we should urge them to implement their moral responsibility *first* by rigorously limiting the occasions for resorting to lying. They should be certain that the cause for doing so is a sufficiently grave cause and not a trivial one. They should compare the proportion of the harm to be avoided to the harm that will be caused by such means. They should foresee some reasonable hope of success. They should lie only as a last resort.

Second, they should restrict falsification to the minimum necessary to secure the justified objective. In particular, they should reject *making a practice* of deceiving the people, for that is the worst possible betrayal of covenant responsibilities. Governments that regularly propagandize their publics, that run all statements through the public relations mill, that use classification procedures to hide their mistakes and deceptions, that attempt to intimidate the free press, that play upon the insecurity and prejudices of the people, are false custodians of the public trust.

Third, they should place the whole conduct of foreign policy primarily in the context of service to the whole national life of the people, and not primarily in the context of instrumental support of national security. To be sure, national security is vital, and foreign policy exists to support it. But the means of maintaining a favorable power balance cannot be separated from their effect on the national society. Therefore, the policy-makers always should be aware of the wholeness of their responsibility. If they are, they will minister to the inner strength of the national community and not subvert it.

The guidelines we have defined for governments in relation to their own people should also govern nations in relation to each other. When the political situation puts the truth in crisis, policy-makers should stringently limit the occasions for and amount of lying and deception. But above all, they should be governed in their actions by the concern to restore, improve, and strengthen relationships of trust, and they should avoid those actions that destroy or permanently impair such relationships.

Invading the Darkness

Jesus told the Pharisees that Moses had allowed divorce "for your hardness of heart," and not because it was the original intention of God (Matt. 19:1-9; Mark 10:1-12). The guidelines we have suggested are necessary because of the hardness of *our* hearts. However, by stressing the importance of covenant obligations and the strengthening of community ties in relation to truth in foreign policy, we have sought to go beyond a mere accommodation to human sinfulness. We have sought to bring the ministry of reconciliation into the midst of political conflict, and thereby to invade the darkness of the old world with the light of the new.

QUESTIONS FOR THOUGHT AND DISCUSSION

1. List the arguments for and against the principle that all agreements with foreign powers should be "open covenants openly arrived at."

2. What limits, if any, should there be to the people's "right to know" what the government is doing in its conduct of foreign affairs?

3. Does a government "have a right to lie to save itself when it is going up to nuclear war"?

4. If you were President, how would you decide a case where you could protect important national interests only by deliberately and seriously misleading the American people?

5. What are the responsibilities of the news media with respect to learning the truth about the conduct of foreign policy?

6. What are your responsibilities?

8 | Christian Contributions to Moral Inquiry

A Necessary Contribution

Throughout this book we have examined different aspects and occasions of moral judgment in foreign policy. We have used the language of politics because we were discussing a political subject. We also have used the language of Christian faith, because the book was written primarily for an audience of confessing Christians. Now the time has come to be even more self-conscious about our Christian orientation. In this chapter, therefore, we shall attempt to summarize and clarify what the Christian faith and the Christian churches can contribute to the process of moral decision in foreign policy.

Discussions of this subject are often short-circuited at the outset because the discussants want to move immediately to the question of whether the churches should "take a stand" on political issues, whether they should pass resolutions, and, if so, whether these should be general or specific. Those are important matters, but they are not the only important matters, and in any event they are not the ones that should be considered first. In fact, the very possibility of taking a stand and passing a resolution presupposes a *process* of thinking together about the problem in question—a process that includes fact-gathering, analysis, clarification, interpretation, identification of responsibilities, and forecast of probable consequences. If our churchly statements on political questions have at times been vague or indecisive or naïve or off the point, part of the explanation surely is that we have not paid enough attention to the process by which we make up our minds as to our moral responsibility.

Our primary task in this chapter is not to talk about how churches should prepare social pronouncements. Rather, it is to ask what Christians—individually and corporately—can *contribute* to the process of moral inquiry, whether the process occurs in the deliberations of a synod or a congressional committee or a League of Women Voters chapter or the National Security Council, or whether it takes place in the mind of a businessman planning foreign investments or a construction worker entering the voting booth or a young man facing military induction.

We assume, of course, that Christians can contribute something. To some persons that suggestion may seem arrogant, and to others it may seem hysterically funny. But we believe it to be true. Moreover, we believe the contribution to be *necessary* to the shaping of a truly responsible foreign policy—one that will see the interests of this nation bound in intimate relation to the needs and rights and aspirations of all the peoples of the world.

What the Christian Faith Can Contribute

The "Other" in Perspective

Situations requiring moral decisions arise only because one party to the conflict has justifiable claims on the resources and actions of the other. If he has no justifiable claims, no moral issue is involved. Or, if one party has no status to press claims against the other, his claims cannot be considered justifiable.

In the Middle Ages the church considered all wars against the infidels to be justified wars. Hence the Turks, being infidels, could not possibly have any justifiable claims against the Christian princes and the other crusaders. The crusaders for their part did not have to wrestle with moral questions on their right to resort to war, nor were they encouraged to limit the means of war against the enemies of God. To the contrary, Roland Bainton argues, "The code of the just war, which was being elaborated and refined by the secular ideals of chivalry and the Church's ideal of the Truce and Peace of God, was largely in abeyance in fighting the infidel. . . . A favorite text was a verse in Jeremiah 'Cursed be he that keepeth back his hand from blood.' " [1]

In our own time, a lawyer for a My Lai defendant explained why his client had willingly murdered Vietnamese civilians, including women and children: "He did not look upon them as human beings, persons with whom he could speak and reason."

Both of these examples show that the sense of moral obligation to the opponent was absent because the opponent was not thought of as having any status to possess rights that would limit the attacker. Unfortunately, intergroup conflict encourages that attitude as a matter of course. That is one of the reasons why moral arguments so often seem irrelevant to those who use power on behalf of groups.

New Testament faith, properly understood and applied, recognizes a status of the "other" that the "merely human view" tends to avoid or reject. It sees the enemy as the neighbor. It sees "the least of these my brethren" as the form in which Christ confronts his disciples (Matt. 25:31–46). Drawing on the Old Testament, it underscores the fact that man—every human being—is created in the image of God. Looking from its own perspective, it sees man, the image of God, participating in the renewal of the world through Christ.

One can truly say, therefore, that Christian faith contributes to the process of moral judgment in foreign policy by bringing the opponent into focus as one whom I must recognize as having the status to impose justifiable claims upon me. I cannot reject his status as claimant without denying his reality as a human being, and I cannot deny his reality as a human being without denying Jesus Christ.

The Self in Perspective

If our Christian faith raises the status of the other in our awareness, it also often lowers our own status. In one respect that is not true: we are "images of God" and beloved of God like the rest of humanity, and that, by the grace of God, is the highest status imaginable. But in other respects our status *is* lowered. The perfect love of Christ shames our self-righteous pretensions and teaches each of us "not to think of himself more highly than he ought to think." (Rom. 12:3) The judgment of God comes to rest upon us, not just upon our enemies, and it breaks our stubborn pride so that we bow in contrition for our sins. The vision of the whole world standing equally in the love of God contradicts our proud presumption that our community has some special status not bestowed upon the others.

Seeing ourselves in this new perspective contributes to the process of moral judgment by encouraging the humility and the openness necessary for moral dialogue. On the one hand, our awareness of our own moral pre-

My country,
right or wrong.

My country, right?

My country?

tensions compels us to test our claims against commonly accepted criteria of justification. On the other hand, our experience of God's grace—in spite of our moral pretensions—enables us to do precisely that.

The Order of Loyalties

Our moral decisions are determined largely by our loyalties, and the crucial moral decisions reveal our ultimate loyalties. To whom or what are we loyal and responsible above all other loyalties and responsibilities?

The modern nation-state makes a powerful claim on the loyalty of its citizens and also of all the groups within its society, including the churches. The tendency of the state is to make absolute claims and thereby to answer the question we have raised by placing its claims higher than any others.

Christian faith historically has recognized the right and the necessity of the state to claim support and obedience from its subjects and citizens. It has thus taken seriously Paul's famous admonition to the Roman Christians, "Let every person be subject to the governing authorities. For there is no authority except from God, and those that exist have been instituted by God." (Rom. 13:1) But by its very citation of that text Christianity has denied the absoluteness of state authority. After all, the authority of rulers comes from God; it is not self-generated. God is above states and rulers. Therefore, when the rulers command something contrary to the will and justice of God, "We must obey God rather than men." (Acts 5:29)

True Christian faith contributes to the process of moral decision in foreign policy by sensitizing the individual conscience so that it both grants the rightful claims of the state and refuses its unjust claims. However, refusal of the unjust claim is difficult for the individual, for he must stand against the massed monopoly of state power, and often he stands alone. In this situation, Christian denominations and congregations ought to support the individual's right to contest the claim of the state on grounds of conscience, even if they do not agree with him in his particular refusal. If the churches forsake this responsibility, they undermine their contribution to moral decision-making and concede all arguments to the omnipotent state. And perhaps more seriously, they abandon those of their children who have taken seriously their teaching to obey God rather than men.

The Order of Values

"For what does it profit a man, to gain the whole world and forfeit his life?" (Mark 8:36) Perhaps the use of the word "soul" rather than "life" in older translations makes the point with more strength, for there is something about the pursuit of values that commits a person for eternity as well as time. The question has a dual significance for foreign policy, which after all is a goal-seeking, value-questing activity. For one thing, it insists on the discussion and clarification of the goals we pursue and the things we value. For another, it demands that we test our political values against a true standard of worth.

We are not sure just how much testing of its values the foreign policy process—or the people who support the process—actually can stand. Do we really value financial investments in sugar plantations and oil fields in foreign countries highly enough to send our sons to die to protect them? Is "world leadership" so clearly our preeminent concern that it is beyond challenge? Is it so important to us not to lose the first war "in our proud 190-year history" that we are willing to prolong indefinitely an otherwise pointless war in support of a corrupt and repressive regime? And here is the showstopper: are the risks of total devastation through nuclear war less objectionable than the risks of unilateral nuclear disarmament?

What does it profit a man if he gain the whole world . . .?

Hopes for History

Moral decisions are influenced greatly by historical expectations. How much time do we have? What do we think we can accomplish? The churches cannot give much clear guidance on these questions, because they often have provided varying answers. At times they have believed the interim before the end of history to be so short that they saw little point in worrying about political decisions. At other times they have seen history stretching out indefinitely before them, but have transferred Christian man's real concern to eternity and left him largely without investment in the practical affairs of states and emperors.

Recent decades have seen the turn of Christian attention toward the life of man in this world. That is the way it should be, for Christ himself came into this world —to redeem it, not to escape from it again. But the act of turning toward the world often has been accompanied by hopes and expectations that seem unlikely to be fulfilled, and in some cases the attempt to fulfill them has been highly dangerous.

That being the case, Christian faith best serves the process of moral inquiry in our time when it offers these two perspectives on history: first, the life of man for the foreseeable future will involve conflict and uses of power.

Conflict may change forms, but it will not go away, because it is an expression of the sinful nature of man. Second, God is present in human history as the power that sustains, corrects, and heals the fallen creation.

The first perspective protects against the shaping of moral decision on the basis of hopes that seem too easy and certain of fulfillment, either by extending the reign of universal law and love or by bringing in the kingdom of God through political revolution. The second protects against the despair of responding to historical challenges by withdrawing from them.

The Limits of Force

We are talking here about moral limits, not practical limits. Morally justifiable force is always limited force. The principal limits are the ones set forth earlier (pp. 55–56) as the traditional "just war" criteria.

If the church is pacifist, its limits forbid any use of force. All uses of force are wrong, and the criteria therefore are inapplicable. If the church is not pacifist, it is obligated to show when and how far force may be justifiable. Eventually that means applying principles to cases. But at the outset, it means informing the Christian conscience as well as the national culture of the existence and relevance of the rules for limiting the use of force.

We should acknowledge, however, that Protestant churches in the United States have performed very badly in this respect; they must bear some of the blame for the fact that strategic decisions as well as battlefield operations have often grieviously violated the just limits of force simply because the persons exercising the force were not properly schooled in their understanding and application. In the wake of the trial of Lieutenant William

Calley, I asked several young men who had held military commissions how much training they had had in the rules of war as they pertained to the refusal to obey illegal orders. Not one could remember having had such training. That is a serious indictment of the armed services. But had I asked them the same question about the moral education provided by their churches, the response almost surely would have been the same.

A misguided form of pacifism has kept some of the denominations from studying and teaching the rules for limiting the use of force, on the grounds that to prepare young men for such decisions in war predisposes them to militaristic attitudes. The result of this nonsense is that when they find themselves under conditions of extreme battlefield stress they are morally unprepared to make the hard decisions forced upon them by the situation. How much responsibility for My Lai and other murders must the churches bear for their failures in moral education? [2]

The Call to National Repentance

An integral part of the church's service for Christ is "that repentance and forgiveness of sins should be preached in his name to all nations." (Luke 24:47) That is also in integral part of the church's service to the nation. Churchmen as citizens view national actions in terms of the nation's interests and their own interests; as Christians they view the same actions in the light of God's Word and his kingdom.

But what does the call to national repentance imply for the process of moral inquiry in foreign policy decision-making? Let us remember that repentance, Biblically understood, is itself a process involving several elements. The principal ones are (1) recognition and acknowledg-

ment of one's sins, (2) sorrow and contrition for one's sins, and (3) turning from one's sinful ways to God for the renewal of life. Each of these elements is morally significant, whether in regard to foreign policy or to any other human activity.

1) "Recognition and acknowledgment of sins" is an occurrence not routinely found in the affairs of states and the interactions of national societies. Relationships of groups to each other are so dominated by pride, defensiveness, and ideological self-certainty, that each group easily deceives itself into believing that it alone is right, that it is always right, and that it never offends against the interests of others. The call to repentance issued by the churches often is the first awareness that something might be wrong with what the group is doing. Such calls are not as a rule gratefully received, but they nonetheless must be sent forth in obedience to the Lord of history and out of concern for those over whom he rules.

2) Sorrow and contrition imply more than just "being sorry we did it." They imply also a recognition of our responsibility to those we have wronged, and that sense of responsibility—as we argued earlier—is the prime requisite of moral obligation.

3) Repentance as turning and as renewal of life involves the determination to break with policies and national attitudes that have led to the destruction of individual and social life, of the fabric of rights and duties, and of nature, and to seek a common ground among the nations for the support of human needs and rights and the control of power.

The church must hold the need for repentance constantly before the eyes of all the people of the nation and especially before those of the nation's leaders, but it must

remember that judgment begins with the household of faith. At the conclusion of World War II, the Council of the Evangelical Church in Germany declared, "We have in fact fought for long years in the name of Jesus Christ against the spirit which found its terrible expression in National Socialist government by force; but we accuse ourselves that we didn't witness more courageously, pray more faithfully, believe more joyously, love more ardently." [3]

The moral failures of the nation in its foreign policy operations are to some extent the failures of the churches. That is partly because Christians as citizens have not brought the resources and insights of faith to bear upon the conduct of the nation's affairs, and partly because Christians as the church gathered have not experienced and proclaimed in its radical character the word of judgment and forgiveness that has been given to them for their ministry of reconciliation.

Advocacy

Finally we return to the question of whether the churches should "take stands" on foreign policy questions. We cannot do it justice in such limited space, but we must say that the culmination of the churches' contributions to moral decisions comes when they make their own commitment. Such statements by the churches are not *as such* outside the province of their responsibility. They are fulfillments of it, insofar as the churches are called to exercise prophetic and educational leadership.

In brief outline, we can offer some suggestions as to how that responsibility is to be discharged. First, the statement should make clear whether it is addressed only to the faithful or to all of society. The theological grounds

for speaking to one or the other should be clear in either case.

Second, the spokesmen should make clear whether they are speaking *to* the church or *for* the church. Speaking *to* the church is an unquestionable responsibility of leadership; it includes the duty of telling the faithful what they don't want to hear but must hear for the good of their own souls. Speaking *for* the church requires unambiguous authorization, but it ought not be the authorization of church "public opinion polls." I agree with John Bennett that "The results of such a poll would hardly differ from a cross section of public opinion in the nation." [4] Therefore, it would not be distinctive of the church. Rather, the authority to speak for the church should come from the church's traditions, doctrines, experience, and informed and representative leadership.

Third, the statement must be in accord with political realities and not with ideal pictures of a world order. Also, it must not insist on moral decisions that do not correspond to the real choices before the statesman.

Fourth, when churchmen have made up their minds through a careful and prayerful process of theological and moral reflection, in the light of the best information available, they should say what they have to say and stick to it. They should not apologize for their action or try to explain away the force of the position taken.

The Presence of the Kingdom

These contributions of the churches, even if adopted and applied faithfully, will not transform the kingdoms of this world into the kingdom of our God. Only the grace of God can do that. But they may help to point to the presence of the kingdom in a world that obscures it both unintentionally and by design. When the kingdom is experienced as present, the new world breaks in upon the old, and man gains a foretaste of the glory that is to come. It is a momentary thing, but it gains continuity in time and extension in space when those who have had the foretaste unite to share in the mission of revealing the new in the midst of the old, and when their unity testifies to the healing power and promise of the one who created them and who makes them whole.

QUESTIONS FOR THOUGHT AND DISCUSSION

1. What is the starting point for Christian inquiries into foreign policy responsibility? Is there a necessary conflict between starting with the Christian message and starting with service to the national interest?

2. Is there anything distinctive about the Christian contribution?

3. What should the churches teach about the limits to the use of force?

4. What should the churches teach about disobedience to unjust laws and to illegal orders?

5. What authorizes church leaders to speak for the church on questions pertaining to foreign policy?

Notes

Chapter 1. Foreign Policy and Christian Faith

1. George F. Kennan, *American Diplomacy, 1900–1950* (New York: Mentor Books, 1952). George Kennan, one of our country's most distinguished diplomats, was on the Policy Planning Staff of the State Department and ambassador to Russia and Yugoslavia.
2. I have done so in my article, "Reconciliation as a Foreign Policy Method," *Religion in Life,* XXXVIII (Spring 1969), pp. 40–54. See also Dieter T. Hessell, *Reconciliation and Conflict* (Philadelphia: The Westminster Press, 1969).

Chapter 2. National Power and Moral Responsibility

1. For a survey and interpretation of the "political realist" position, see Kenneth W. Thompson, *Political Realism and the Crisis of World Politics* (Princeton, N.J.: Princeton University Press, 1960).
2. Ambassador Kennan assigns morality the role of "gentle civilizer of the national interest." Despite the seeming implications of his argument, he has a strong sense of moral responsibility concerning the conduct of foreign policy.

   For more on this subject, see Arthur Schlesinger, Jr.'s article, "The Necessary Amorality of Foreign Affairs," *Harper's,* CCXLIII (August 1971), pp. 72–77.
3. See Arnold Wolfers, "Statesmanship and Moral Choice," in *Discord and Collaboration* (Baltimore: Johns Hopkins, 1962). Also, Hans J. Morgenthau, "The Mainsprings of American Foreign Policy: The National Interest vs. Moral Abstraction," *American Political Science Review,* XLIV (December 1950), pp. 833–854.

Chapter 3. A Humanly Sensitive Foreign Policy

1. See Michael Novak's treatment of "sensitivity" and my response in *"Story" in Politics* (New York: Council on Religion and International Affairs, 1970).

2. George F. Kennan, *Memoirs, 1925–1950* (Boston: Little, Brown & Co., 1967). This incident reveals another side to Kennan's thought about the relationship of morality to foreign policy than the one referred to in Chapter 2, p. 34.
3. *Ibid.,* p. 151.
4. This problem is discussed by J. J. Servan-Schreiber in *The American Challenge* (New York: Avon Books, 1967).

Chapter 4. Giving Reasons for Our Violations

1. Text from *The Atlanta Constitution,* May 1, 1970.
2. i.e., not a *legal* argument, even though the President is an attorney.

Chapter 5. The Role and Limits of Intervening Force

1. For a good discussion of the "lessons of Vietnam," see Edwin O. Reischauer, *Beyond Vietnam* (New York: Random House, 1967).
2. *The Korean War and Related Matters, Report of the Sub-committee to Investigate the Administration of the Internal Security Act and Other Internal Security Laws to the Committee on the Judiciary,* United States Senate, 84 Cong., 1 Sess., January 21, 1955 (Government Printing Office, Washington, 1955), p. 7. Quoted in Dean Acheson, *Power and Diplomacy* (New York: Atheneum, 1962), pp. 35–36.
3. See the treatment of this problem in my *Modern War and the Pursuit of Peace* (New York: Council on Religion and International Affairs, 1968). Also, William V. O'Brien, *War and/or Survival* (Garden City, N.Y.: Doubleday, 1969), Ch. VII, "Revolutionary War and Intervention."

Chapter 6. Communism and Reconciliation

1. Barry M. Goldwater, *Why Not Victory?* (New York: Mc-Graw-Hill, 1962), p. 120.

Chapter 7. Truth in the Public Squares

1. Quoted in William J. Barnds, *The Right to Know, to Withhold and to Lie* (New York: Council on Religion and International Affairs, 1969), p. 23.
2. For an excellent discussion of this matter, see Harold Nicolson, *The Evolution of Diplomacy* (New York: Collier Books, 1962).
3. John Spanier, *American Foreign Policy Since World War II,* 3rd rev. ed. (New York: Frederick A. Praeger, 1968), pp. 168–169.

4. John M. Blum, *Woodrow Wilson and the Politics of Morality* (Boston: Little, Brown & Co., 1956), pp. 141–142.

Chapter 8. Christian Contributions to Moral Inquiry

1. Roland Bainton, *Christian Attitudes toward War and Peace* (Nashville: Abingdon, 1960), p. 112.
2. Telford Taylor's *Nuremberg and Vietnam: A Challenge to America* (Chicago: Quadrangle Books, 1970) is a very useful study of the problem of disobedience to illegal orders.
3. From "The Stuttgart Declaration," reprinted in Franklin H. Littell, *The German Phoenix* (Garden City, N.Y.: Doubleday & Co., 1960), p. 189.
4. John C. Bennett, *Foreign Policy in Christian Perspective* (New York: Charles Scribner's Sons, 1966), p. 155.